*Is Christ
the End of the Law?*

Biblical Perspectives on Current Issues

HOWARD CLARK KEE, General Editor

Is Christ
the End of the Law?

GERARD S. SLOYAN

THE WESTMINSTER PRESS
PHILADELPHIA

First edition

Published by The Westminster Press®
Philadelphia, Pennsylvania

PRINTED IN THE UNITED STATES OF AMERICA

1 2 3 4 5 6 7 8 9

Library of Congress Cataloging in Publication Data

Sloyan, Gerard Stephen, 1919–
    Is Christ the end of the law?

   (Biblical perspectives on current issues)
   Includes bibliographical references and index.
   1. Grace (Theology)—History of doctrines. 2. Man
(Christian Theology)—History of doctrines. 3. Law
(Theology)—Biblical teaching. 4. Jesus Christ—
History of doctrines—Early Church, ca. 30–600
5. Law and gospel—History of doctrines. I. Title.
II. Series.
BT761.2.S63   230   77–27454
ISBN 0–664–24190–5

CONTENTS

Editor's Foreword   7

Introduction   9

  I. Deliverance and Torah   15

 II. The Law in the Teaching of Jesus   38

III. Is Christ the End of the Law?   70

IV. Beyond the Synoptics and Paul   107

 V. Greco-Roman Influences   124

VI. The Church Fathers Set the Course   134

VII. Implications for Contemporary Faith   153

Notes   183

Scripture Index   197

Subject and Author Index   204

EDITOR'S FOREWORD

Many Protestants find themselves in a self-contradictory position. On the one hand, they deplore the lack of a sense of moral responsibility in our society, especially among the free-wheeling youth culture. On the other hand, they think that one of the major gains growing out of Vatican II and the ecumenical spirit of Pope John XXIII is that "at last the Roman Catholics have caught on to the Pauline doctrine of justification by faith."

Dr. Gerard S. Sloyan, distinguished New Testament scholar, knows Paul well, and understands profoundly his teaching about justification. But as a Catholic scholar, trained in that tradition of the Law and the structures that God has built into his creation, he is equally at home in the realm of Christian moral—even legal—responsibility.

This learned and comprehensive study strikes a superb and rare balance between the meaning of grace and the meaning of moral responsibility. It should serve as a valuable corrective to the mindless "do your own thing" dogma that has inflicted the latter part of the twentieth century. It also helps to put in perspective the biblical concept of grace, that reconciling, transforming power which is not merely taught in the New Testament but became incarnate in Jesus Christ. The thoughtful reader of this book will perceive how the appropriation of these realities has given balance and structure to the ongoing life of the church.

HOWARD CLARK KEE

INTRODUCTION

The gospel of Jesus Christ was first preached on Jewish soil in late antiquity. Believers in the gospel as a revelation of God see in it and in its central figure, Jesus, a religious uniqueness. Yet they do not hesitate to explore the circumstances surrounding its birth and growth, its abortive career in the Jewish world, and its remarkable spread in the Greco-Roman world.

In the Jewish milieu, where it might have been expected to flourish as a Judaism with a faith and practice for gentile God-fearers, it failed lamentably. Only recently do we begin to get satisfactory studies on the Jewish origins of Christianity.[1] On the other hand, many volumes have been produced that attempt to show the interaction between the earliest Christian movement and its pagan environment.[2] Clues to the current positions of Christianity in faith and ethics are sought by inquiring into what it drew initially from the Greek and Roman worlds.

The present book will concern itself with a few fairly simple matters. They are chiefly the relationship between, or the identity of, the gracious action of God in the person of Jesus Christ and his covenant Law delivered to the Hebrew people. A corollary to this will be the measure in which, if at all, the Christian message can be expressed by law. A second matter of interest in these pages will be whether God's gracious action in the world can be characterized as a second order of activity distinct from the primary order of nature

and a "natural humanity." What, in other words, is to be
thought of the creation in the light of redemption, and vice
versa?

This book does not assume that God acted differently than
before in the career of Jesus and what followed from it. As
preparation for the central inquiry, it will ask some questions
about the religious outlook of the Middle East—specifically
the Jewish outlook of the two centuries 150 B.C. to A.D. 100.
In this Jewish world, the Mosaic Law came to be central for
most Jews, but not for those we know of who followed Jesus.

How did the Jewish people and the peoples around them
view the universe and humanity's place in it? What was
thought of the cosmos, of the world of nature? How did the
human family relate to the world that was its home, to fash-
ioning a life for itself before God, to sex and marriage, to
death? Did the person of Jesus or what was made of him in
the preaching of the gospel constitute a difference in these
matters? If so, what was influence and what influenced? Did
Christianity shape the late ancient world or was it shaped by
it? And, whichever the case, what was the measure of that
influence?

The questions raised do not, at first blush, seem to revolve
around "simple matters." Law and grace is as profound an
issue as was ever dealt with by Judaism or Christianity. The
same is true of grace and nature.

The Jew is long familiar with a Christianity that has defined
him or told him what Jewish faith ought to be. These pages
will try to avoid that pitfall. They will have task enough in
examining the Christian situation. There, the conventional
wisdom on the two problem areas of inquiry—law and grace
and nature and grace—is so firmly fixed that it may seem
presumptuous to disturb it. The Christian thinker tends to
say that Christianity is fully at ease in the cosmos, and that
a dispensation of superabounding divine favor fulfilled one of
covenantal promise after an interim of law. Our question is,
are both statements true?

It is clear from the Hebrew revelation that all that God

made was good. The heavens are the work of his fingers, the moon and stars orbs he has set in place. All sheep and oxen, beasts, birds, and fish in the sea have been given to man to "rule," have been "put under his feet" (Ps 8:3–8; cf. Pss 100:3–5; 119:73).[3] Whoever the human creature is, he is—at least for the psalmist—"little less than the angels" and "crowned with glory and honor."

Already in this sketch of Hebrew harmony there is tension. To speak of dominion over the subhuman universe is to suggest that this creature so high on the scale of creation may not be thoroughly at ease with himself. He loves his role of eminence too much. How does humanity fit into the cosmos for Christianity as a coordinate or subordinate member? In another line, what is humanity's normal condition if its graced or restored condition after redemption in Christ has about it a certain abnormalcy? Or, if that restored situation is normal, what was abnormal about all the millennia that preceded it?

At the root lies the profound tension between a Creator and free creatures other than himself. There is the conventional satisfaction taken by Christians that they, along with Jews and Muslims, accept the cosmos as God's creation and do not despise it. The Hebrews were grateful for the universe, while worshiping none of it. The Christians differed from them on this in no particular. At an early period they met the challenge of radical metaphysical dualism posed by gnostic thought and overcame it, both in official statements and largely in practice.[4] The major exception is in the realm of sexuality and the low value put on it by the preference of virginity and celibacy to marriage.[5]

Yet many who are not Christians (and some who are) are by no means sure that the victory has been achieved. They are convinced that Christianity won the battle but lost the war, that it went over to the enemy it assumes it conquered. This is thought to be true in so many matters that a difference between the dualism of the gnostics and that of the Christians is held to be barely discernible.

Another conventional Christian position is that, from the human point of view, the God of love proceeded in act from the privileged moment of creation to that of the transmission of the Law and thence to his self-revelation in Jesus Christ. With the Lord's return in glory there will be the consummation of all. In none of these stages is God less than gracious to the human race or to his chosen people. Yet the third or Christian epoch is featured as so abundant in grace and reconciliation that a shadow is inevitably cast on the first two.

The explanation usually proffered is that the creation was vitiated by a primordial fall; the Law was interpreted as a final settlement when it was meant to be provisional; the graciousness of God in Jesus Christ outran all former bounds.

Still, weighty problems remain. With the "fullness of grace and truth" that came with Jesus Christ, a period of little grace and truth apart from him seems to be assumed. The Jesus who taught an intimacy with God and world was made the mediator to a distant God and the sign of opposition to "this world." He was hailed as the author of a realm of grace so total that, for practical purposes, Christians began to live in a two-sphere universe, the redeemed world of grace and the world of sinful nature.[6] "Precisely," say some Christians. "Not so," say others, "but one world ameliorated by the fullest outpouring of grace in the final age."

It is no wonder that the non-Christian is unsure of what he sees when he looks at the Christian phenomenon. It is equally understandable why Christians are uncertain over what they see when they look within their own tradition. Their seamless garment of faith has been rent many times—notably in the West since the late medieval period—by disputes over these matters. A basic cleavage over God's grace in Jesus Christ and the power or powerlessness of human nature lay at the heart of the sixteenth-century split in the West. Reformers found that Catholics were wedded to "works of the Law," while Catholics responded that humanity was "deprived, not depraved" and that fidelity through Law observance could be a positive good.

Overall, the positions taken by Catholics, Orthodox, and Protestants on these subjects are sufficiently diverse, and still at such odds with the Jewish teaching from which all derive, that a close examination of the Christian stance on law and grace and nature and grace seems very much in order. It shall be attempted in the pages that follow.

Chapter I

DELIVERANCE
AND TORAH

Because it is commonly held by Christians that with Jesus
Christ there came a divine dispensation of grace succeeding,
or even, as many would have it, replacing, one of law, it is
important to explore how the ancient Jewish world per-
ceived God's grace or gracious action. This exploration
should include an inquiry into the relationship between the
Law of Moses and the Abrahamic covenant, and also the
concepts of salvation and redemption. A preliminary inquiry
should likewise be made into the way in which Jewish
sources, chiefly the Bible, conceived the cosmos and the
world of nature vis-à-vis the way they viewed a world in
which their God, the LORD, was active in Israel's behalf. Only
then can we say what difference Christianity made.

The question, Is Christ the end of the Law? requires a
careful examination of the meaning of Law in the Hebrew
Scripture and other Jewish writings. The Jewish religious
experience going back to the exodus or to Abraham was not
interpreted in the same way by all Jews. The Jewish world
into which Christianity came was extremely diverse, and the
fact of that diversity is easier to recognize than are the precise elements of which that diversity consisted.

There were numerous writings that gave clear indications
of various interpretations of the Jewish religious experience
in the time of Christian beginnings. A collection of works in
an apocalyptic vein, called the Apocrypha and the Pseudepigrapha,[1] were known to certain New Testament writers, and

represent the thought and piety of Jewish communities of
the time.

THE RELIABILITY OF THE SOURCES

The scrolls from the Dead Sea communities of Qumrân,
which can be dated from roughly 100 B.C. to A.D. 68 or 135,
have enlarged our horizons about the kinds of Judaism that
were abroad in the days of Jesus and the early spread of the
gospel. These biblical books and fragments of books, commentaries, and writings proper to the sect, inform us chiefly
about a non-diaspora Judaism. It was apocalyptic and moder-
ately dualist, yet passionately Jewish. The great figure of
Qumrân, the Righteous Teacher, like John the Baptist and
Jesus, leads us to wonder how many other charismatic leaders
there might have been who did not fit into the rabbinic mold.
The Torah was of supreme value to the Righteous Teacher,
yet he did not view it in anything like the spirit of the rabbis,
with their many opinions of the binding force of individual
commands and precepts. There was also an opposition to the
Jerusalem temple in the scrolls like that reflected in the NT.

The Dead Sea finds provided us with an immense advance
over what had been known from the Damascus Document
discovered in Cairo in 1896 and the descriptions in Josephus
and Philo of the Essenes and the Therapeutae respectively.[2]
The augmented information provided by the scrolls should
make us cautious about assuming that we possess adequate
information on the Pharisees, the Sadducees, and the Zealots
in the brief descriptions of each given by Josephus or in the
allusions to them in the gospels.

The only NT case in which the problem of contemporaneous witness to the actual situation does not arise is in the
authentic epistles of Paul. These were written in the 50's and
perhaps early 60's. We have no reason to deny Paul's claim
to be a zealous Jewish observant at an earlier period (Gal 1:
14), a Benjaminite and "Hebrew of Hebrews, as regards the

law a Pharisee" (Phil 3:5) in his young manhood. Jewish readers may be unhappy with Paul's self-perception and even
more with the way he departs from a rabbinic tradition that
is coming into being. This is no reason to deny the way he
sees himself, nor to say that he is by definition an inauthentic
claimant to the mantle of Pharisee or rabbi. The standards for
authenticity were not yet fixed when he wrote. Therefore we
shall not say that Judaism taught this or that in Paul's time,
because we cannot be sure of any such consensus. All that we
can say is that Paul taught as he did without entertaining any
scruple about its being Jewish.

We have to draw a blank on two important matters. First,
did Paul assume that the recipients of his letters had a large
amount of knowledge of Bible and extrabiblical legendary
elaborations (cf. Gal 4:22–26 = Gn 16:15; 21:2; 17:16; 2 Cor
3:13 = Ex 34:33ff.; 1 Cor 10:1–5 = Ex 13:21; 14:19–22; 16:
4–35; 17:6; Nm 20:7–11; 14:16), or only what he has brought
to them in his previous teaching while with them? Secondly,
we cannot know what if any is the Jerusalem origin, or even
the Jewish origin, of the many opponents of his gospel and
ministry whom he identifies in his epistles (cf. Rom 16:18–20;
1 Cor 6:12f.; 2 Cor 11:13ff.; 12:11; Gal 3:14; 6:12; Phil 3:2f.).[3]
His definitive "mission to the gentiles" is a construct of Lucan
theology (cf. Ac 18:6). He himself does speak of evangelizing
the uncircumcised as his special calling (cf. Gal 2:2, 7f.). Yet
from his letters alone, he seems to be fully in touch with
fellow Jews throughout his career.

Regarding the opponents to his ministry, Paul writes that
"certain ones who came from James" inhibited Cephas' meal
behavior at Antioch (Gal 2:11–14). We cannot with any certainty extrapolate from this the sure existence of a "Judaizing
party" of which one hears so much. The "Judaizers" are a
hypothesis of scholars, a cipher that may stand indiscriminately for Jews, for Christian Jews of the James party, or for
syncretists who have incorporated some Jewish practices into
their systems. In sum, just as the exact influence of diaspora
Judaism upon Paul's career escapes us on the evidence of his

letters, so does the measure of interference with his activity by local Jewish congregations, by delegations of religiously observant Jews, or by observant Christian Jews from Judea.

There are other important areas, however, about which we can speak with relative certainty. They are matters such as Jewish agreement on the goodness of creation, on the primordial sin of angels and men, and on the effects thereof; also, God's gracious love for Israel expressed in covenant and Law, and the ways in which he expected a return of that love. The basic statements from the time of Christianity's beginnings are biblical, with a certain supplement from apocryphal and sectarian sources. Commentary on the Bible had begun and may already have been abundant, both orally and in writing. Much of it was to be codified later as the Mishnah and the Talmud. Many of the important biblical statements are contained in the five books of Moses, edited during or shortly after the return from the exile (ca. 535 B.C.).

MYTHOLOGY A MINOR MOTIF

In earliest times Israelite religion was marked by certain mythological elements which subsequently faded, although not every vestige was eradicated. The unique feature of biblical religion was its affirmation of one sovereign God. He had neither consort, peer, nor pedigree. There is no myth of his origins. Environment does not seem to account for this religious outlook. Israel's immediate neighbors were imaginatively polytheistic. They had numerous myths about the births of their gods. Israel cannot be termed primitive in any scientific sense, as if at an earlier stage of development. There was an Israelite lapse into idolatry attested to in the Bible, and Israel's God, YHWH, has mythological features, but, overall, mythologism is not a major motif.

YHWH wins no victories in a cosmic struggle with other gods. His worshipers merely topple their idols. When he is described as supreme over the sea monster Rahab, or Tannin the dragon, or Leviathan, these traces from Ugaritic mythology simply show his supremacy over Yam, the chaotic sea, and its inhabitants. All is spoken of as taking place "in ancient times" but well after the creation. God is never in a struggle with primordial divine powers. It is always a struggle with his own creatures, who, like the snake in Gn 3, reflect "the demonic realm as a whole."[4]

The demons in the Bible are never deposed deities, any more than the angels of the preexilic period are gods reclassified as servants of YHWH. Both phenomena are without exact parallel in religious annals. There are two sets of messengers of YHWH who do his bidding, angels and demons ("messengers of evil," Ps 78:49, including Satan, who in Jb 2:1 is a member of the heavenly court). Neither angels nor demons are transmuted deities. Angels are but a nameless "host" doing God's will (at least before the exile, after which came Michael, Gabriel, and the others).

THE SOURCE OF EVIL

The demons need to be accounted for on some other principle. Close examination of the biblical Satan, the serpent of the garden, and the "giants" of Gn 6:4 reveals that evil is localized in each case in individual rebellious wills (the moral realm), not antagonistic cosmic forces (the realm of being). What lies behind Jewish demonology is sin. Hence Satan becomes the tempter and seducer of humanity. He is never promoted to the level of an opposite metaphysical principle to God.

The advantages of restricting evil to the creaturely are immediately apparent. In the order of being, all that exists is attributable to YHWH, not to some rival cosmic power. He remains supreme over chaos in human life, since he is the cause of its cause. Disordered wills, angelic and human, are responsible for the profoundest human ills, including otherwise inexplicable natural disasters and the misfortunes that plague individuals. This is the positive side of biblical demonology.

Its negative side is the possibility of legendary proliferation. While in principle YHWH is the source of all, including the demonic, the very positing of such a class of refractory creatures leaves the door open to mythical elaborations. Thus, Satan progresses from his role as the adversary of humanity to that of the chief of the devils and then leader of the fallen angels who took human wives. His illicit offspring beget every kind of magic, necromancy, and divination. There is, in other words, an unseen host of anti-God forces as active as God in the human community. The isolation of evil to the ethical realm is preserved, but barely. With the growth of legends about the devils and their powers, the door is opened to what may well be understood in popular religion as a countervailing metaphysical principle to the divine. This admits the possibility of a dualism, however "moderate," sanctioned by the religion itself. One may choose God as the utterer of all curses (the position favored by the Genesis author) or attribute evil to creatures as if they were its principle.

Israel has a cleaner bill regarding the neutral and even good quality of matter. God did not make the heavens or the earth, the sun or the moon, out of preexistent stuff. We are left to conclude from Gn 1:1–2 that darkness and water and a water-covered earth were made first, then separated in orderly fashion. No one but God is the maker of anything. "He suspends the earth over nothing at all" (Jb 26:7). No force in nature comes to birth from a god or is beholden to one for its continuance. The displays of nature such as storms, fire, and clouds may serve to highlight YHWH's self-disclosure in the world, but he does not need them. He controls nature and is not controlled by it. No "bond of life and destiny" is to be found between the forces of nature and God. He draws strength from no power-filled objects. All objects are equally his servants, manifestations of his will and power. There is no bridge between the created universe and God.

The only exception to the above generalization is certain superhuman beings translated as "sons of God" or "giants," a deified, celestial race of men (cf. Gn 3:5; 6:1-4; Ex 22:19; in 1 Sm 28:13 the same Hebrew word is used to describe the spirits of the dead).

The legends of Gn 1-11 account for the origins of various evils such as death and pain, murder, violence, and idolatry. The story of Adam's free choice with regard to the fruit of the tree is meant to account for the origin of sin. From the beginning of human history rebellion was possible. Adam proved unequal to the test and by his disobedience disclosed the realm of evil that had been hidden from him. Death began as a result of this sin, along with other hardships. Humanity did not lose freedom with the first sin, but with it the proliferation of evil began (cf. the Cain story, Gn 4:1-16; the preliminary to the Noah story, 6:5f.).

This, in general, was the state of Jewish thought on matter and sin as Christianity came to birth. There was no second realm alongside the divine. God's grace was known as the basis of creation, whatever creation's chaotic or flawed condition. For the latter, conscious rebellious choice was responsible, not any other god or force. From the beginning of the history of the cosmos (which Israel saw as of a piece with *its* history), angels and humans had defied God and brought evils down on their heads. Things were as they were in a troubled universe because creatures would not serve God. They were free and should obey. It was the role of the later prophets to envision a final judgment when human rebellion would come to an end.

GOD'S DEED OF DELIVERANCE

Central to the Mosaic books was the story of the LORD's determination to save his people. "Save" is used in the literal sense of delivering them from extermination in Egypt and death in the desert. This deliverance is the most basic meaning of salvation in the Bible: the actual saving of the lives of Jews as a people and individually. No other divine act takes precedence over it. The call of Abraham may be considered the founding event of the Jews as a people; the call culminates on Sinai in the creation of a covenant community, with its terms of life in the new land for a people recently saved.

The LORD proffered a sign at the bush that he meant to be with the Israelites. When Moses brought the people out of Egypt they would "worship God on this mountain" (Ex 3:12), the Horeb of Moses' experience (v. 1). The exodus narrative is a tale of God's resolute will to deliver his people from their otherwise hopeless condition. Such is his grace of salvation toward them. The release from bondage which the LORD promised at Horeb proceeds on schedule. Moses, with his wife and sons, returns from Midian to Egypt (4:20), with Aaron as Moses' designated spokesman (vv. 14ff., 28). The two brothers convince their elders of Moses' message from the LORD (vv. 29f.). They go off to Pharaoh to demand freedom so that this people can have a feast to their God in the desert (5:1). The political situation of the Hebrews grows worse (vv. 2, 10–13, 21), until Moses is assured by the LORD that Pharaoh will act, "forced by my mighty hand . . . and outstretched arm" (6:1).[5]

The directions for avoiding the fate of the Egyptians in the final plague belong to the oldest literary source, according to Otto Eissfeldt.[6] The explanation of the rite of Passover, described as a "perpetual ordinance" (Ex 12:24), is contained in the proposed response of the presiding male to the children present. This continues to be a part of the order of service on the great night of deliverance: "This is the Passover sacrifice to the LORD, because he passed over the houses of the sons of Israel in Egypt when he struck down the Egyptians, but saved our houses" (v. 27). The commemorative meal is to recall forever God's gracious act of salvation.

The deep impression made by this deed of deliverance never passed from Jewish memory. It became central to the songs and liturgies of this people. Perhaps the best-known record of the event occurs in the chant of Ps 136, the "Great Hallel." The antiphonal phrase, "For his great love is without end," occurs twenty-six times in response to individual lines of praise such as, "He brought Israel out from their midst," and, "With mighty hand and outstretched arm."

COVENANT AND TORAH

There are numerous traditions about the legal codes of the Hebrew Bible and just as many about the covenant. Theories abound on how each developed to reach its present form in the edited books. Yet there is widespread agreement that the tradition on deliverance from Egypt preceded that on the giving of the Torah. God's saving of his people had to precede the principles by which the community might be guided. *At the heart of the relationship of the LORD and Israel is the concept of covenant.*

The much-edited book of Genesis recounts its pre-history. It begins when God looks at everything he has made and finds it good (Gn 1:31). He then makes a suitable partner for the man (2:18–24), who has named all the cattle and birds and wild animals (v. 20). After the flood, he promises Noah that never again will he doom the earth because of man (8: 21f.). Of this the rainbow in the clouds was the sign (9:13–17). The covenant was offered to "all flesh," i.e., all mortal creatures (v. 17). This phrase later impelled the rabbis to extract from the five Mosaic books seven basic precepts, called Noachide (Noachian), which, according to Jewish authorities, even the gentiles had to keep.

Beginning in Gn 12 there occur various expressions of covenantal intent on the LORD's part to act graciously toward Abram and his offspring (Gn 12:2f., 7; 13:14–17; 15:1, 5f.). A covenant is ritually "cut" after sundown in answer to Abram's question, "How am I to know that I am to possess [the land]?" (15:8). The answer is given: "To your descendants I will give this land, from the Wadi of Egypt to the Great

River [Euphrates] . . ." (vv. 17–21). The covenant is repeated
in Gn 17:1–8 to include the change of Abram's name—"the
father is exalted"—to another form, Abraham; folk etymol-
ogy sees the extra syllable as connoting "father of a host [of
nations]" (v. 5). The requirement of circumcision as a sign of
the covenant is recorded in this passage (17:9–14, 23–27).
After Abraham has trusted in the LORD and shown himself
ready to sacrifice his son, the covenant is repeated (22:17f.)

The promise is narrowed down, after Abraham's death, to
Jacob over Esau (Gn 25:23; 27:27ff.). Jacob wrestles with a
mysterious stranger at Peniel ("face of God") and afterward
has his name changed to Israel, which is explained as a play
on the verb "contended" (32:29; cf. 35:10). Under his new
name he hears the covenant renewed by God and sets up a
memorial shaft there (35:11f.), naming the site Bethel
("house of God," v. 15). The old man Jacob-Israel lives on in
Egypt with his influential son Joseph to the age of 147 years
(47:28). He dies pronouncing oracles on all his sons, with a
special blessing on Judah from whom the scepter shall never
depart (49:8–12). Joseph, in turn, dies in Egypt at 110, re-
minding his brothers: "God will surely take care of you and
lead you out of this land to the land that he promised on oath
to Abraham, Isaac, and Jacob" (50:24).

The LORD identifies himself to Moses as the covenant God
at Horeb, as he instructs him to remove his sandals (Ex 3:5f.).
Moses' son is circumcised in haste as he approaches Egypt (4:
25). The LORD repeats the identification while sending
Moses off to face Pharaoh: "I am the LORD. As God the
Almighty I appeared to Abraham, Isaac, and Jacob, but my
name LORD I did not make known to them. I also established
my covenant with them, to give them the land of Canaan, the
land in which they were living as aliens. . . . I will take you
as my own people and you shall have me as your God" (6:2ff.,
7a). The people released from Egypt are therefore a covenanted people from first to last.

In the Bible the covenant concept is unilateral from the
side of the LORD. He is this people's sovereign king. His

relationship to them is one of benevolence and affection. There is nothing contractual about the covenant; it may not even be called a compact between two parties that bind themselves. He is on record regarding what he means to do for his people. He is not looking for slavish obedience or obsequiousness, merely an acknowledgment that he is who he says he is, namely, "I AM" (Ex 3:14). The people must reverence him as "the LORD, the God of your [Moses'] fathers, the God of Abraham, the God of Isaac, the God of Jacob."

This covenant concept was present before there was Torah. When Torah came, through delivery on Sinai, nothing was altered. "The indispensable and loving instrument holding the community of God and Israel together is the law."[7] Later the rabbis would state that the whole world was created for Torah, that it was the ground plan of the universe. But, as Abraham J. Heschel points out, "it is not law and order itself, but the living God who created the universe and established its law and order, that stands supreme in biblical thought."[8] This convicts all who seem to praise the Law as if it were ultimate. Only God is ultimate and the Law a sign of him.

LAW AND LIBERATION

Basic to the divine initiative regarding Israel was God's will to liberate. He is described as saying: "You will know that I, the LORD, am your God when I free you from the labor of the Egyptians and bring you into the land which I swore to give to Abraham, Isaac, and Jacob. I will give it to you as your own possession, I, the LORD" (Ex 6:7b–8). The grace and mercy of God constitutes Israel a free people, free to worship the God who describes himself as "I AM."[9] The basic agreement of the relationship was that the people would heed God's voice and keep his covenant (Ex 19:5–6a; cf. Gn 17:7f.). Beyond their accepting deliverance from bondage at his hands and being saved from thirst and starvation, God's only demand was that he be acknowledged.

With the speaking of the Ten Words (Ex 20:2–17), the terms were offered whereby the people would not be slaves to selfishness, greed, and passion in the new land. This was the covenant with the God of their salvation made specific. It laid down basic principles of cult and ethics. It told a people how to respond to God's love in trust. The God who identified himself on Sinai as the giver of covenant terms (Ex 20:2; cf. Dt 5:6) was a liberator and a life-giver. The preface to the giving of Torah contains no mention of the promise made to the fathers starting with Abraham. Yet the covenant renewed on Sinai during the exodus bore the strong imprint of immediately past historical events.

This people was related to its God, and its members to one another, through conformity to commandments as an expression of gratitude. The Law was itself a form of grace, a graciousness first expressed in the creation, then in God's dealings with all who preceded the patriarchs. The gift of Torah for maintaining a loving relationship with him was an out-and-out gratuity, a covenant that was an "uncovenanted blessing."

From first to last the covenant was beneficent, a deed of condescension from One highly placed to others humbly placed. In the ancient world, law stipulated as much of what we would call love as that world knew. Law assured justice in a milieu where the suffering of the oppressed derived from a lack of justice. No greater grace could come to those released from bondage than a series of social settlements which assured that they would not shortly be returned to bondage. By keeping the Law they could not enslave themselves to themselves. Fidelity to it in the new land would literally be a choice of life, as Deuteronomy was later to stress: "Loving the LORD your God, heeding his voice, and holding fast to him will mean life for you, a long life for you to live on the land which the LORD swore he would give to

your fathers Abraham, Isaac, and Jacob" (Dt 30:20). Keeping
the Law, Moses said in that same reported valedictory, is "no
trivial matter for you; rather, it means your very life" (32:47).

The observance of the sabbath, which the Genesis author
related to God's rest after the creation (Gn 2:1–3), was for the
Deuteronomist a reminder of the grace of deliverance: "You
shall remember that you were a slave in the land of Egypt,
and [the LORD] your God brought you out with a mighty
hand and an outstretched arm; there [the LORD] your God
commanded you to keep the sabbath day" (Dt 5:15). Hence
on every sabbath Israel was to remember that its God was a
liberator who had put an end to all slaveholding. Rest from
work was to remind the people of the freedom they had
already been given. "The sabbath commandment shows in
an especially instructive way that the basic commandments
are a great gift to Israel to help and benefit her. Far from
being demands, the Commandments are exactly the opposite: they free Israel from demands."[10]

THE PROPHETS AND THE LAW

It has frequently been said that the prophets of the eighth
and seventh centuries were the founders of the tradition of
"ethical monotheism" as we know it. Julius Wellhausen could
write: "The prophets do not speak out of the Law but out of
the spirit; [the LORD] speaks through them, not Moses. Their
torah is worth just as much as that of Moses and issues from
the same perennial source."[11] Wellhausen insisted that he
espoused no theory of evolutionary development of dogma
but one of real progress in revelation dictated by events. Still,
his bias in favor of "spirit" and against "law" is fairly clear.
Both Torah and prophecy were, for Wellhausen developments subsequent to the founding of Israel as a community
in the time of Moses. Part of the argument in favor of his view
is the fact that the definitive formulation of the idea of the

covenant does not come before the sixth century. In the form in which we have it in the Bible it is a product of the period of the exile.[12]

The opinion held in the earlier part of the twentieth century that the prophets were opposed to the Law seems to be, however, largely spent. It is now generally agreed that the prophets accepted Mosaic religion as their religious heritage and intended merely to reform it. Their concerns were ethical, to be sure. But at root they favored a return to the ethics of Torah, which they saw widely flouted in the two Jewish monarchies around them. They deemphasized the covenant terms, it is true, but they were not ignorant of the covenant, whatever impelled them to play it down. Perhaps their criticism of monarchy was responsible, with its shift from a covenant between the LORD and the community in Moses' time to one between the LORD and David (cf. 2 Sm 7:16; 23:5). It could well be that the authors of the prophetic books refused to use the word "covenant" too often lest they seem to be granting the case of the monarchy. That institution held that the Davidic throne (later, that of Omri and his successors in the north) had by the divine design preempted the former relationship between the LORD and his people. The prophets, for their part, were incurably committed to the prerogatives of the LORD and convinced that the monarchy threatened those prerogatives.

Concerning the Mosaic covenant, they defended against violation and neglect the basic tenets it proposed. They pointed to God's benevolence as something that preceded the people's ingratitude and disobedience. The prophets looked on ethical goodness as the correct response to the ten commandments. When they resisted temple sacrifice they did so insofar as it was being viewed as a substitute for just behavior. Likewise they associated history with moral demands, which certainly was the Mosaic tradition. The prophets were critics of political events in both kingdoms on the basis of an older covenant tradition. They largely ignored the covenant claims of the Davidic arrangement lest they seem to be either agreeing to it in practice or attacking the LORD in theory.[13]

Our purpose in this brief summary is to emphasize that the word Torah in the biblical context of the covenant means something like teaching, guidance, or instruction. In the five books of Moses it is total in its application. No aspect of life escapes it: worship, property, hygiene, relationships with non-Israelites, marriage, and family. It is a scheme for the total dedication of life to the LORD. Frequently it is said that the word Torah does not mean law. But that observation is often addressed to Christians who are prejudiced against the Law. To be sure, there is much in the five books of Torah besides the Law—narrative, genealogy, history, deeds of power. Nonetheless, the Law is at the center.

The Law is the gracious act of God whereby his revealed will becomes known to his delivered people. Israel has been saved once for all in being brought out of Egypt. To maintain its saved condition Israel must express its gratitude for God's saving and sustaining acts. Torah shows the way. A network of precepts and ordinances is the form it takes. That form is expendable, as the huge body of rabbinic accommodations and the several major types of modern Judaism make clear. The underlying reality, however, is not expendable. The LORD expects that this people will be faithful to him through a lived life. Setting his "spirit" against the Law as if it represented some higher good is not biblical, since only through the power of his spirit was the Law revealed and only by his powerful breath sustaining the people or an individual can it be kept.

There is no fully worked out theory in the Bible of how God enables anyone to obey him, nothing at least that is similar to a Christian theology of assisting grace. This silence does not mean that the idea is absent. All of Jewish life is graced life, from the first day of creation to the present moment. The God of Israel as "spirit of the LORD," uncreated Grace itself, is constantly at work. The gracious deed of creation is followed by the promise of graciousness to all human-

ity in Noah, and again in Abraham. The choice of the patriarchs leads to the choice of a people, constituted "my
people" by covenant in the exodus event. The transmission
of Torah is a great grace. Corresponding to it is the human
power in freedom to keep it. The biblical God is never por-
trayed as setting Israel to commandments it cannot keep.

Whatever problems Paul and other Christians had with the
purpose of the Law, or human hardship in fulfilling it as it was
interpreted in their time, they could not accept the Bible as
expressing a revelation and deny that Torah was its core. On
any reading of the biblical books, the two were one. Revelation could not be set against law, nor law against revelation,
neither by the prophets nor by Jesus and Paul. As we hope
to see later, the problem the Pharisees set out to solve was
how to interiorize Torah, just as it was the problem of Jesus.
Neither had any intention of denying or dismantling it. The
Pharisees did not opt for external observance and Jesus for
internal. They chose two different ways of total fidelity.

Jacob Myers has compiled an interesting set of texts in
which the prophets of the eighth century are seen upholding
the ten commandments; there are texts against idolatry (Is 1:
4; Hos 4:17; 8:4; 13:2), sabbath-breaking (Am 8:5, the only
such text), dishonoring father and mother (Mi 7:6), murder (Is
1:15; 5:7; Hos 4:2), stealing (Hos 4:2; 7:1), adultery (Hos 4:2;
7:4a), and covetousness (Is 5:8; Mi 2:1f.). The theme of the
prophetic books continues to be: The LORD has not broken
his word, his covenant; the people have broken theirs.

The seventh-century prophets who led up to the Josian
reform continued to see in the offenses of their times viola-
tions of the Law. Thus, Zephaniah fulminates against princes
and judges, prophets and priests who have done violence to
Torah (Zep 3:4). The youthful King Josiah hears the book of
the Law, newly found in the temple, read out to him by the
scribe Shaphan, who in turn got it from the high priest Hil-
kiah (2 Kgs 22:10f.). He rends his garments and commands
the priest to teach the people the stipulations of this book,
since the LORD has been angered by the failure of "our

fathers" to observe its words (v. 13). Josiah attempts to be another David, a religiously reforming imperialist, and it costs him his life. He renews the covenant with the LORD (2 Kgs 23:3; cf. 2 Chr 34:32a), "covenant" understood both as the terms of this book (Dt 12–26 and 28–30, in all probability) and the LORD's offer made to Israel. The latter is the Sinai-Horeb event. The setting of the story in 2 Kings is a call to repentance and amendment of the life of a people that had forgotten the LORD's grace and goodness to their fathers. The Deuteronomic reform is a return to former ways, when Torah was central in people's lives. There was no hesitation to recast the story of the first four books to meet the exigencies of the present age. The author employs the Hebrew verb root for "love" twenty-three times, a usage he may have derived from Hosea. Only in Deuteronomy of all the books in the Pentateuch does God's love for his people appear in that expression. The Deuteronomist stresses God's love again and again in order to motivate his contemporaries to repentance. He finds the exodus-redemption motif fundamental (e.g., Dt 5:6; 6:20ff.; 10:12ff.; 26:5ff.) and uses the covenant concept throughout to convey God's relationship with Israel.[14]

Jeremiah takes up the covenant language of Hosea, but only once mentions the LORD's love for Israel. The strong Deuteronomic emphasis on love as the basis for election is wanting. Yet the term "to know" is frequent in the covenantal sense, if not the explicit sense of Am 3:2: "You alone have I known of all the families of the earth." When the new covenant is inscribed on people's hearts, "all of them shall know me, from the least of them to the greatest" (Jer 31:34). Second Isaiah speaks of covenant a half dozen times but not in reference to the events of Sinai. The old covenant, only a shadow of things to come, will yield to an "everlasting covenant" (cf. Is 55:3 and 61:8; this is a common term in the Priestly writings, although there is no specific reference to the covenant at Sinai). The everlasting covenant will be a covenant of peace. In Ezekiel, himself a priest, the terms kindness, fidelity, and insight of former books become stipulations and judgments (Ezek 11:19).

ZEAL FOR THE LAW IN LATER WRITINGS

The later historical works—Chronicles, Ezra, and Nehemiah—are marked by new zeal for the Law, but the covenant idea continues in force to keep legalism from taking over. The emphasis on the Law is due to a determination to take the LORD's demands so seriously that the covenant relation might remain unimpaired (cf. 2 Chr 33:8; Neh 10:8; 13: 8). Thus the Torah was not an instrument of salvation—that had already happened—but a set of principles reflecting the state or quality of a saved people.

In the Priestly writings, the Law had been viewed as an offer of the LORD followed by acceptance. The cultic sacrifices were prescribed so that a relationship with God might be maintained, not achieved for the first time. The Holiness Code of Lv 17–26, which seems older than the Priestly and Deuteronomic elements it fuses, seems to bear this out. For 1 and 2 Chronicles the Davidic covenant is paramount (cf. 1 Chr 17:11ff.; 22:9; 28:4ff.; 2 Chr 21:7). Still, the author is aware of the Abraham covenant (cf. 1 Chr 16:14ff.; 2 Chr 30: 6) and is familiar with the importance of the saving events of the past (cf. 1 Chr 17:21f.; 2 Chr 6:5; 7:22). The books of Ezra and Nehemiah restore the historical basis of the covenant which Chronicles seem to lack (cf. Neh 9; Ezr 9:6–11).

Keeping the Law of the LORD comes to have a new importance in these writings which it has not had previously (cf. 1 Chr 22:12; 28:7f.; 2 Chr 6:16f.; 7:17–20; and 33:8, where fidelity to it is a condition of protection for David's successors). Ezra the scribe is spoken of as having "set his heart on the study and practice of the law of the LORD" (Ezr 7:10), a venture in which the king of Persia supports him (v. 26). In recasting the "memoirs of Nehemiah," the Chronicler insists on fidelity to "the commandments, the statutes, and the ordinances which you committed to your servant Moses" (Neh 1: 7ff.). Ezra's promulgation of the Law of the Lord over the course of a week (cf. Neh 8) is connected with the purification of the land by the dismissal of foreign wives (cf. Ezr 9:12; 10: 44; Neh 10:29ff.; 13:23–30). Priests and Levites are restored to regular temple service (cf. Neh 12). The ancient prohibitions against work and commerce on the sabbath are reinvigorated (cf. Neh 13:15–22). This renewed emphasis on the Law was an attempt to avoid interruption of the terms of the covenant offered by the LORD, so faithfully would his demands be kept. Israel's election led to observance. Observance was never thought to be the basis of election.

It is frequently said that the new zeal for the Law in the postexilic period led to the legal direction taken by later Jewish life. A commonplace in Christian scholarship asserts that whereas the Law formerly expressed the covenant relation, in a reversal of the old order "it now becomes the condition of its restoration."[15] The case can perhaps be made for the seeds of such a mentality. But in the fourth-century evidence that we have (1 and 2 Chronicles, Ezra, Nehemiah), the covenant idea is still in control of legal observance rather than controlled by it. The earliest stratum of talmudic materials (enshrined in the Mishnah of the first two centuries A.D.) attributes to Ezra the scribe certain prescriptions of the rabbis. The latter cannot be thought of as active until after the Maccabean revolt and the Hasmonean priest-kings, on the basis of any extant evidence. Only then, probably, did the scribes begin their careful attention to the precepts of the Law as an alternative form of covenant fidelity to the daily sacrifices of the temple.

LAW IN THE WISDOM LITERATURE

A certain ambiguity exists in the wisdom literature, compiled after the exile, with regard to the place of the Law in Jewish life. The general setting is covenantal, but references to keeping the Law are few (cf. Prv 19:16; 28:4–7; 29:18; Eccl 12:13; Jb 23:12; cf. also Prv 15:8; 21:7 on the sacrifices of the wicked). In their place is praise for sapiential teaching (cf. Prv 1:8; 3:1; 13:14; Eccl 8:2, 5). There is likewise some reference in the deuterocanonical books to obeying the Law (cf. Wis Sol 2:12; 6:4; Sir 2:15f.; 7:27–31; 35:1; 45; 49:4), while chs. 11–19 of the book of Wisdom are an elaborated homily on the exodus from Egypt. The covenantal name of God, YHWH, is widely used. Overall, the authors seem confident that their teaching is a heavenly wisdom that sums up the demands of the Law.

There is much discussion as to whether the meaning of the Hebrew word for covenant was changed by the Greek noun used in the Septuagint. The original meaning of "divine dispensation" may be altered by "testament," which would somehow involve the death of the testator to make it operative. Yet the Septuagint word has one clear advantage: it does not convey the notion of a bilateral pact obliging both parties, as the rejected cognate would be more prone to do. The ambivalent word for covenant in the Bible describes on the one hand legal regulations obeyed to ensure God's continued care and on the other a divine benefit having little or no element of reciprocity.[16] It is probably correct to say that the word chosen by the Septuagint translators inclined the New Testament writers to view the covenant as a testament or divine deliverance primarily rather than as a set of terms expecting fulfillment (cf. Mt 26:28; 2 Cor 3:6; Heb 7:22; 8:6; 9:15, 20). In the "covenants" of God (Rom 9:4) it was God alone who set the conditions.[17]

LAW IN THE EXTRACANONICAL BOOKS

The two books of Maccabees declare the identity of the "covenant with the fathers," the Law, and the precepts of the Law, for all practical purposes (cf. 1 Mc 2:50ff.; 2 Mc 1: 2ff.; 1 Mc 2:20f., 27; 1 Mc 1:57). The challenge to break individual laws is taken as synonymous with repudiating the covenant relation (cf. 2 Mc 7:37). Elsewhere in the deuterocanonical writings, Tobit praises prayer and fasting and identifies almsgiving as freeing from death (Tb 4:10f.; 12: 8f.). Good works are praised as saving in 2 Bar 51:7 and as a treasury of righteousness (Test Levi 13:5; Naph 8:5; 2 Bar 14: 7), but not in Bar 2:19 of the second or Greek canon. There it is said: "Not on the just deeds of our fathers and our kings do we base our plea for mercy in your sight, O LORD, our God." A passage in 2 Esdras, probably from a pre-Christian source embedded in a post-Christian work, falls somewhere in between: "And every one that shall [then] be saved, and shall be able to escape on account of his works or his faith by which he has believed, such shall survive from the perils above-mentioned and shall see my salvation in my land" (2 Esd 9:7). The Assumption of Moses, the first-century A.D. work of a pious Pharisee, puts the two elements of God's gracious initiative and obedience to the commandments together. Moses speaks to Joshua:

> < The LORD > has on their behalf [viz., the nations of the earth] appointed me to < pray > for their sins and < make intercession > for them. For not for any virtue or strength of mine, but of his good pleasure have compassion and longsuffering fallen to my lot. . . . Those who do and increase the commandments of God shall increase and be prospered; but those who sin and set at nought the commandments shall be without the blessings above-mentioned, and they shall be punished with many torments by the nations. (Asmp M 12. 6–7, 10–11.)

The Dead Sea scrolls material has a certain legal orientation, but prophetic and apocalyptic elements are far from absent. Basically, the community's writings reaffirm and renew the one covenant of God and Israel.[18] Absolute trust in the Righteous Teacher is required. It will result in salvation through a community that calls itself "the covenant" or "the new covenant."

The exodus events continue to be important for the earliest stratum of rabbinic materials.[19] Gradually (we cannot know how gradually because the editing work on Mishnah and Talmud were only beginning) there is a change of emphasis. Whereas exodus and covenant are at first central and the Law is but its terms, the Law comes to be the major matter as that which sums up all the demands made by God on a covenanted people. Conforming to these terms appears to be the first priority. The gift of the covenant that lies behind them seems to recede. The distinction between means and ends has become confused. Fidelity to the covenant principle has been obscured by conformity to precepts, ordinances, and commandments. With this summation we come into the period of the origins of Christianity, careful to avoid the generalization (for which there is no solid evidence) that a legalist spirit had supplanted the earlier concern with Torah as the sign of a covenanted existence.

Rabbinic Judaism attempted successfully to reverse the trend of Hellenization which had been strong in Jewish life since the death of Alexander the Great, and especially since the rule of the puppet Hasmonean and Herodian houses. This Greek influence was a reality in the diaspora and in Palestine almost equally. There was also a wide variety of Jewish practice that had as its chief points of focus the priesthood and the Law. Some groups, such as Qumrân, were deeply committed to Torah but in nothing like rabbinic fashion. There was also widespread opposition to the Jerusalem temple cult.[20]

SUMMARY

Since there was no single fixed canon of Scripture in the Jewish world into which Christianity came, and since apocalyptic writings in Greek had wide currency, along with commentaries of limited circulation such as those found in the Dead Sea scrolls, the following things seem clear:

—The deepest reality of Jewish life was the status of the people as a community to whom its God, YHWH, had given a covenant out of gracious love.

—The chief expression of God's covenant love was the Law delivered on Sinai. The priests had been its teachers until recent times, when a learned class known as the scribes had risen to teach fidelity to its accommodated individual precepts as the best means of response to God's covenant love.

—There was concurrently a widespread expectation of vindication at God's hands in the imminent "final age." The two chief expressions of this hope were sporadic armed revolts and an apocalyptic (revelatory, visionary) literature that did not propose military action.

—Despite lively descriptions of "the end," Jewish life had not lost its firm grip on reality, on the goodness of the world, or on human freedom as the means by which response had to be made to God's gracious overtures.

—A strong current of demonism was abroad in Jewish thought.

—Whether Jews followed messianic hopefuls in armed uprisings, the teaching of the scribes, or charismatic figures such as the Righteous Teacher, John the Baptist, and Jesus, all alike were committed to fidelity to the covenant expressed through the Law. The modes of interpretation varied widely, however, from radical commitment to the main intent of the Law, to updated accommodations of its hundreds of ancient precepts.

Chapter II

THE LAW
IN THE TEACHING OF JESUS

The first three gospels were written by persons who thought that God's deed in Jesus Christ made an immense difference. But did this difference include—as Christians commonly say —an end to the importance of the Law of Moses, and even of all law as a way to know God's will? Did the evangelists, by their interest in the fairly immediate coming of the end of days, invite followers of Jesus to an active disinterest in this world and its demands? And was there a "spiritualizing" of human affairs in the gospels that was uncharacteristic of the biblical books? These are the questions this chapter must face.

There is widespread assumption in the church that the gospel of Jesus Christ supplanted the Law of Moses. The death and resurrection of the Lord inaugurated an age of grace that succeeded one of the Law. In it the literalism and particularism of Jewish existence gave way to the spiritualism and universalism of Christian life. These positions, so widely held as almost to have the force of dogma, deserve examination. If they prove not to be true as stated, there is hope for a viable relationship between Jews and Christians heretofore impossible. Moreover, the possibility of the survival of Christianity as a world religion, at least in the view of this author, will be greatly strengthened.

The chronological search into Christian origins begins properly with Paul's epistles. The first of these—1 Thessalonians—was written about A.D. 50. But researches into the hypothetical Q, the sayings collection in Greek that Luke and Matthew seem to have had in common, indicate that it too may have been circulating in the year 60 or even 50. The same is true of the narrative elements and non-Q sayings found in Mark. Mark's is the first gospel properly so called—sayings and narratives both—to be written, about A.D. 70. Similarly, the Greek original of the sayings collection that appeared in Coptic in the Gnostic library of Nag Hamâdi, Upper (i.e., southern) Egypt, in 1945 could well have existed in primitive, pre-Gnostic form by 50 or earlier.[1] The scholarly consensus is that Jesus' sayings in this Gospel According to Thomas—which, having no narrative elements, is not of the genre gospel—exist in even less developed form than Q, which in turn undergoes modifications as Luke and Matthew adapt it to their purposes.

WHY BEGIN WITH THE SYNOPTICS

This chapter will examine law and grace and God's relationship to the world as presented in the synoptic gospels of Mark, Matthew, and Luke. We begin here, not because of some assumed priority of the gospel material over Paul's writings but for reasons that have to do with the history of the church. The church never presented in the gospels an "authentic" or historical Jesus, neither as to his deeds nor his words. Rather, it always presented an interpreted individual viewed as an object of faith. In the Catholic and Orthodox traditions, and in Protestantism largely, the faith portrait of Jesus Christ in the gospels has been accepted as being on a par with that of Paul and the other writings. Often the tensions that exist between Paul and the first three gospels, and other books as well, were disregarded. Not until F. C. Baur raised the issue early in the last century did the major dissonance between Petrine and Pauline, Hebraic and Hellenist elements—as he identified them—surface. This led to more than a century of New Testament research, largely by Protestant scholars, who tended theologically to prefer the Pauline presentation of the gospel to that of the evangelists.

In recent decades Rudolf Bultmann has claimed that the synoptics were preparatory to the proclamation of the message of salvation. According to him, the church's full proclamation about Jesus as Lord and Christ first appeared in Paul and John. To this has been joined Hans Conzelmann's idea of a "canon within the canon." This judgment sees a greater importance in Romans and Galatians, for example, than in Luke-Acts and Revelation. The parentage of the idea is to be found in Luther's conviction that certain NT books were barely evangelical or, like James, unevangelical.

A poor view of the three synoptics does not mark Protestantism generally, it should be noted. Still, the emergence of Pauline theology as the purest expression of Christianity because of its stress on justifying faith has left its mark. The Catholic and Orthodox churches, while professing Christian faith of a Pauline type, tend to put the gospel accounts of Jesus' words and deeds on a par with Paul's theologizing without attempting to reconcile the differences in the two approaches. The Catholic tradition retains a concern for the legal which is often branded "Jewish," while John Calvin restored to the tradition that bears his name a full-scale respect for biblical ethics. This came as part of his teaching that the Hebrew Bible was no less binding because no less inspired than the NT.

The fact is that the three synoptic gospels were much more influential on Christian thought and writing up to the year 200 than were the epistles of Paul. Readers who suppose that Pauline thought is Christianity and vice versa are normally surprised to discover the absence of Pauline teaching in the extracanonical Teaching of the Twelve Apostles (The Didache), Hermas' Shepherd, or Justin's Dialogue with Trypho. It is true that 1 Clement (ca. 100) and Ignatius of Antioch (ca. 110) know the primary, secondary, and tertiary Pauline letters, but it is not until after these are received into the canon about 175 that Paul begins to exert a major influence. Widespread acceptance of John's gospel comes even later. Second-century Christianity is, above all, Matthean, when it is not argued straight out of Genesis, Isaiah and other prophets, and Psalms. This early and never interrupted concentration on Jesus' own teaching, edited as we know it to be from the viewpoint of church life, accounts largely for the present decision to deal with the gospels first.

A second reason is the quite recent discovery, through redaction or composition criticism, that none of the evangelists, not even Mark or the author of Q, operated without a clear theoretical purpose. Each had a theology of Jesus as the Christ and as savior, the latter unmarred in Q by the absence of a passion narrative. In Q's outlook, Jesus is the bringer of salvation in the final age. Since Mark is not the mere compiler of wonders and sayings for a biographical purpose that he was thought to be fifty years ago, the Christianity of Mark, Q, or Greek-Thomas may have been the whole of Christianity for some believers. The same is true for the churches of Matthew, John, Luke, and James. They were not waiting for a Paul, of whom the first two had probably not heard, to tell them what Christianity was in its fullness. They thought they knew.

Consequently, the synoptic and other non-Pauline witnesses need to be heard on what human and earthly reality is, and grace and law and sin. A church that accepts an inspired canon of twenty-seven books must attend to each document singly, since the various authors supposed that their works proclaimed the saving message with total adequacy.

Finally, Paul's teaching on law and grace does not resemble that reported of Jesus in any gospel tradition. Not even John's teaching attributed to Jesus on new "life," which comes closest to Paul's, resembles Paul's gospel in all respects. In canonizing Paul's epistles the church did not designate that his doctrine was superior to that of the other apostles. It merely acknowledged his vigorous claim to the title of apostle and said that he had written under inspiration. Becoming a gentile church early, the church came to appreciate in a special way Paul's claim to work for the gentiles (cf. Gal 2:8, supported by Ac 13:46). His arguments, which seemed to disparage Jewish claims regarding the way of salvation, were hailed, while his support of an eventual vindication of the Jews (Rom 9–11) was treated as a kind of curio of the consummation of the age. Only recently has the church begun to realize that its theologians of special devotion, Paul and John, have been responsible for much intense anti-Jewish feeling—whatever their intent. So long as its apparent stance against the Jews as God's people goes unresolved, the church cannot continue to make faith claims touching the entire human race. The gospels of Matthew and Luke (-Acts) and the epistles of James, 2 Peter, and Jude in particular provide a balance to John and Paul. Since Matthew and Luke-Acts are thought to support the triumph of anti-legal gentile Christianity, an examination of them should prove extremely helpful.

Some questions that arise are: Do the synoptics contain a teaching which holds that spirit is opposed to matter? Is the world to come set against this one which is under Satan? Is grace in Christ the antithesis to life under the Law? Whether large numbers of Christians can remain faithful to their own tradition, and whether the gospel can be preached effectively throughout the world hinge on the answers to these questions.

MARK

Howard Clark Kee has argued convincingly that Q has but two pieces of narrative material (Lk 4:2b–12; 7:2–3, 6–10) and three of hortatory nature which have no reference to the future (Lk 16:13; 11:33–36; 17:3–4, 6).[2] The remaining forty-seven Q passages he establishes as eschatologically oriented. Many of these are ethical in tone, as are the three above, but always with a view to judgment in the future as God's reign is brought to consummation.

Mark's gospel shows Jesus to be a wonder-worker in a successful contest with demonic powers. The struggle remains cosmic, yet there is internal evidence that a previously existing "divine-man" cycle has yielded to the concept of a suffering "son of man" in the present gospel. Jesus is "son of God" as well for Mark, an ambiguous title which connotes divine choice for a task but not full divine status. His glorification will come about only through real suffering in the body. This contrasts strongly with the thoroughgoing dualism of the Coptic Gospel of Thomas. In Thomas, "wretched is the body" (87); "whoever has found the world has found a corpse" (56); and Jesus marvels that "this great wealth [spirit] has made its home in this poverty [body]" (29).

Mark is "otherworldly" in the way that all Jewish eschatology is. In the coming age Mark expects that this world will be renewed, the good vindicated, and the wicked subjected to punishment. He believes strongly in a world of "unclean spirits" and in the power of God vested in the man Jesus, who, even in this age, overcomes them. Jesus heals and restores in Mark. His ministry replaces disorder and chaos with well-being and peace. He does not call into question the materiality of human existence but assumes it and tries to overcome its fragmented character.

Many of the sayings in Mark have futurist reference, but they can be construed as an ethic for a present of some duration. They do not deny present reality in favor of a future eon which is viewed as the sole reality. The exchanges over sabbath observance, on the oral Law on utensils, and on written Torah on kosher laws (Mk 2:1–3:6) bear traces of what could have been real debates in Jesus' lifetime. The gentile character of the intended readership is evident in that Mark is little bound by Mosaic observance as the rabbis were coming to enunciate it. He reports conflicts on Law observance as if they occurred in Jesus' lifetime, with pointed reference to his own milieu. Mark's Christians hold to Torah but not in terms of rabbinic interpretations then current.

The question of which sayings of Jesus are likely to have

been historical will not be explored here in detail. The gospels present the Christ of each evangelist's faith and hence of the church's faith. To discover that faith portrait of Jesus Christ is to identify the primitive Christian spirit. The historical Jesus was never made the test.

The Gospel of God

Mark's church is committed to an order of grace known as the reign of God. Opposed to this reign are "unclean spirits" —evil intelligences whom Jesus addresses (Mk 1:24f.), who blaspheme against the Holy Spirit and cannot expect forgiveness (3:29). The reign of God has begun with the Baptist's preaching, but its completion lies in the future. Meantime, the successive "little apocalypses" of Mark culminate in testimony placed on Jesus' own lips as to who he is (14:62) and to his being raised from the dead (16:6). The final word of the young man at the tomb to the women who came to anoint Jesus' body is: "Go, now, and tell his disciples and Peter, 'He is going ahead of you to Galilee, where you will see him as he told you'" (v. 7).

The "gospel of God" is Mark's title for the marvelous but pain-filled career of the Jesus he knows as the Christ. It inaugurates an order of grace. This gift is unearned although it had long been awaited. It can be considered Israel's due only as the consummation of the covenant promise, which in its totality is in an order of grace. The reign of God will succeed the present age but is not yet a reality. The life, death, and resurrection of Jesus is a presaging of this reign, but his disciples cannot enter it until they endure his sufferings. His being with them in Galilee is probably a parousial reference—viz., to the final consummation on the last day.

Jesus is a teacher in Mark who assumes that his hearers have the power to obey God freely. The anthropological understandings are completely Jewish. People live in an order of grace because God is their creator, redeemer, and teacher. They can and must do what he commands to avail themselves of his promises. No special help is indicated to avail a person of new life in God's reign. The mere preaching of it assumes the power of the hearer to heed and follow.

"The tradition of the synoptic gospels as a whole," writes Walter Schmithals, "is not favorably disposed to the Law, but constantly defends the Christians' open-minded attitude toward it, partly in the form of controversies with the Pharisees."[3] The first part of this judgment is widely assumed to be true. But is there in the synoptic tradition any positive interest in rabbinic attitudes toward the Law? Undoubtedly in collecting Jesus' sayings and editing them in a polemical spirit the Palestinian Christians were aware of their thrust against the reckoning of reward and against self-satisfaction from having done what was legally correct. Jesus' recorded sayings resemble pronouncements in the Talmud against certain types of Pharisees. Yet Jesus cannot, on the evidence of the earliest stratum of sayings, be understood to have opposed the entire Pharisee tradition of observance.

Mark's transmission of the two commandments of love for God and for neighbor—"there is no greater" commandment than these (Mk 12:31)—was clearly intended to show that Jesus was a better interpreter of Scripture than were his contemporaries (cf. vv. 28–34; Mt 22:34–40). Notice also that this passage is placed between passages about the nature of the resurrection (12:18–27) and the substitution of the concept of David's "Lord" for David's "son" (vv. 35ff.). In all three, Jesus' eminence as an expositor of the Bible or traditions that had sprung from it is highlighted.[4] The linking of Dt 6:4f. and Lv 19:18 inevitably emerged as a foundation stone of Christian ethics because it was invested with the authority of Jesus. Yet it is not featured elsewhere in this gospel. Rather, "the Markan ethics is one of discipleship."[5] "Coming after me" (Mk 8:34; cf. 1:17), "losing one's life for my sake" (v. 35), and "not being ashamed of me and my doctrine" (v. 38) summarize the chief ethical demand of Mark. To follow Jesus clearly embraces suffering ("deny himself," "take up his cross," v. 34) and extends to "anyone," not just to "the Twelve" of 3:16–19.

Jack T. Sanders, quoted immediately above, is among those who hold that Mark has no ethics whatever besides those of a final age soon to come. He says that Jesus teaches nothing here of how his followers are to deal with one another, only of the way they are to watch and wait (cf. Mk 13:33, 37), enduring persecution (cf. 8:35–38). This reduction of the commands of Deuteronomy and Leviticus to the zero point seems unacceptable, since the joining of the two seems a positive assessment of two basic, non-eschatological matters in Mosaic teaching, one of them deriving from the recited daily prayer of Dt 6:4.[6]

The Law Still Binding

We can only conclude from the direct quotations from the Law in various parallel synoptic passages (Mk 12:29ff. = Mt 22:37ff. = Lk 10:27; Mk 10:19 = Mt 19:18f. = Lk 18:20) that observing the words of the decalogue continues to be a matter of importance to Christians.

Mark's Christians do not view the Law in the Marcionite sense of its being in no way binding. The Jews and gentiles for whom the synoptic gospels were written are convinced that they have a new freedom from the Law's dietary prescriptions but are not unanimous as to its extent. Thus, Mk 7:19*b* and Ac 10:15 reflect the view that no one is bound, in the latter case not even Peter, while Matthew consciously omits Mark's phrase, "Thus did he declare all foods clean." Luke does not have the passage in any form. Likewise not held binding are those teachings of the oral Law which touch on table fellowship (Mk 2:15ff. and parallels); working (Mk 2:23–28 and parallels; cf. Mt 12:15, which refers to a technical violation of the sabbath permitted to the priests commanded to sacrifice in Nm 28:10); and healing on the sabbath (Mk 3:1–5 and parallels).

We have reported the opinion that the placement of the "great commandment" in Mark (12:28ff.) signified his interest in this saying for its christology rather than for its ethical implications. The second-century church thought the summary a matter of ethical importance to Jesus. The primary ethical thrust of Mark may well be eschatological discipleship. Still, the post-Jewish church was little attuned to eschatological thought. It took Mark's injunctions to watch and wait (13:33, 37) as connoting readiness for death through good living rather than an impending last day. That the author of a gospel was interested only in eschatological repentance, and not in any program of conduct touching this world or the people in it, would have surprised second-century Christians. It probably would have done the same for those of the first century, who read about discipleship and thought it had to do with right living in the present—eschatological expectation quite apart.

Mark's major concerns may have much to do with making sense of the recent destruction of the Jewish temple and capital. Mark marshals the traditional materials at his disposal to present a Jesus who teaches Galilean or Antiochene Christians what they are to make of the debacle in Jerusalem. The recent events are taken by him as anticipatory of final events. The exact measure of Jesus' eschatological concern is something we cannot know. Mark's concern is such that his gospel (ch. 13 in particular) is probably a late-first-century apocalypticizing of Jesus' teaching.[7] The similarity of its details to Josephus' account of the destruction of Jerusalem contributes to this impression.

This Age and the Next

In Mark, Jesus' followers are to be engaged in mutual service, even as he came to serve and give his life (Mk 10:42–45). They are to continue in an eschatological table fellowship which is covenantal like that commanded of old (14:24; cf. the wording of the two miracles of the loaves, which reflects community meal behavior: 6:34–44; 8:1–9, 14–21). The divorce regulations of Dt 24 are challenged (Mk 10:2–12) in a compassionate move in regard to women. A catalog of vices to be avoided, such as those with which Jewish and Greek cultures were familiar, is given (7:21f.). What the Law pro-

hibits is included purposefully for Christians (10:19). Despite
Mark's consistent gaze toward the eschatological future (un-
derscored in 14:62 and concluding with the allusive 16:7), he
is not unmindful of the force of the Law regarding this covenant community. The chief concern of his believers is to
watch for the end while enduring trial, yet they know what
they must do in the interim. In his lifetime Jesus seems to
have recalled certain obligations of the Law and set others in
perspective in his concern for the Law's deepest demands.
Mark's church felt bound to the interpretation of the Law
given by the Teacher (14:14). How long it would bind this
"faithless generation" (9:19) no one knew, not even Jesus (13:
32). But it continued to be binding.

The word "grace," meaning God's favor leading to an improved condition for humanity, occurs much in Paul and
occasionally in Luke-Acts. It is not found at all in Mark or
Matthew. The latter two employ the term "the reign of God"
(Matthew, often "of the heavens") to convey the idea. This
reign is God's doing. It will overtake people in his good time
—suddenly, swiftly, without warning. Humanity's task is to
trust that it will come and that they will be ready. Jesus, in
preaching the reign of the God he called Father, assumed
that obedience to his will would best ensure its coming.
When this kingship of God arrives, it will be in continuity
with all that has gone before. The parables of Jesus stress this.
It will not be a new life for the race but the fruition of the
old one. God's gracious conduct toward his people will continue as it began: in benevolence, in justice, in mercy.

This means that salvation as Mark and Matthew proclaim
it lies in faith in God's power manifested in Christ, in learning
God's wisdom from the Teacher, in doing his will in loving
obedience. In Mark, Jesus' death is a shedding of his blood of
the covenant which was to be poured out on behalf of the
many (Mk 14:24; Mt 26:28 adds "for the forgiveness of sins";
cf. Mk 10:45). If the reign is to come in its fullness, there must
be adherence to the Law understood correctly. In a word,
there is a renewed order of grace that consists in obedience

to the Law rightly understood. No distinction is made between the call to discipleship of Jesus and a capacity to answer it. Later theology will see in the life of grace in Christ an order of existence so far above the human that special assistance or new capacities are needed if anyone is to dwell in it. In Mark, the God who issues the call is the gracious Father of the human race. Following Jesus closely will lead to life in the reign of God after the time of judgment. The mystery of the life that leads up to this is uninterruptedly of a piece with Israel's covenanted life with God.

MATTHEW

"Do not think that I have come to abolish the law and the prophets. I have come, not to abolish them, but to fulfill them" (Mt 5:17). This may have been a saying of Jesus. It is more probable that Matthew formed it with some such understanding as that Christ is the end of the Law (cf. Rom 10: 4). Matthew is also probably the framer of v. 20, which proposes a "righteousness" for Jesus' followers superior to that of the "scribes and Pharisees." It serves as an introduction to the antitheses that follow (vv. 27–48). These summarize, in a variety of transcending interpretations, the ways in which Christians are to keep the Law. Thus, the saying is critical of current interpretations of the Law familiar to Matthew but holds for a right way to keep it. It proposes love as the better righteousness.

There is nothing specifically Christian about vv. 18 and 19 of Mt 5 (cf. 1 Clem 27:5; Mk 13:31). They contain a rabbinic axiom about utter fidelity to the Law phrased in two ways. In taking it over, Matthew is underscoring his conviction that the ultimate sense of the Law is brought out through Jesus' interpretation of it. Such is the sense given to these Jewish commonplaces about legal observance. "To fulfill" means for Matthew to establish the will of God completely. His theology sees in Jesus the one dependable expositor of the Mosaic deliverance. The school of Iavneh was coming to the fore in his day, proposing accommodations of the ancient legal corpus in the spirit known as *halakah* ("the path"). Matthew agrees with these rabbis that the Law must be kept, whether by Jewish Christians or any who venerate the books of Moses apart from Jesus. He is no friend to an antinomian spirit, represented by the "false prophets" he warns against in 7: 15ff. and 24:11ff. He wants observance that will lead to righteousness, observance of the new and better kind that comes from following the interpretations of Jesus.

It is not important whether Matthew was the first to take over the axioms of 5:18–19 and give them a Christian meaning or found it already in the tradition. It is more probable that it is he who has accommodated these watchwords about the Law to a Christian purpose. By his series of contrasts between "the commandment imposed on the ancients" (v. 21) and "what I say to you" (v. 22) Matthew makes two things clear: he is neither a Christian Jew who feels bound by the emerging rabbinic consensus, nor a Marcionite before his time who sees no relationship between the gospel and the Mosaic dispensation. There is such a relationship. There must be fidelity. He chooses the middle ground of what he considers perfect observance in a new spirit.

Christ, the Law's True Interpreter

Jesus submits to John's baptism in Matthew's gospel "to fulfill all righteousness" (3:15). This is an important value to this evangelist, but as has been pointed out, it is a "higher righteousness" (5:20) he has in mind. Matthew's Jesus engages in a tirade against the "scribes and Pharisees" for their modes of observance of the Law which do not pursue the true righteousness which is the Law's intent (cf. ch. 23). The Law is of great consequence to Matthew, as witness his phrase put on Jesus' lips, "everything I have commanded you" (28:20), a verb that contains the sensitive noun for "commandment." But it is the Law as expounded by Christ, its one true interpreter.

This is part of the larger Christian conviction that, whereas Scripture is God's inspired word and for that reason authoritative (cf. Mt 1:22; 2:15; 12:26; Ac 1:16; 4:25; 2 Cor 6:16–17), Jesus Christ and he alone is the key to the understanding of Scripture. Jesus can put aside Mosaic permission for divorce (cf. Dt 24:1) by citing Gn 1:27; 2:24; 5:2. In Mt 5:38 he directly contravenes the ancient principle, "An eye for an eye and a tooth for a tooth" (Ex 21:24; Lv 24:20; Dt 19:21). Since the whole mentality of the NT authors is that "scripture cannot be broken" (Jn 10:35), they think that the Law has to be kept in Jesus' spirit or a spirit consonant with faith in him. This must have appeared to the rabbis who had other convictions about observance to be precisely the opposite of keeping it.

There is no antinomian spirit regarding the past in any of the synoptic gospels (cf. Lk 16:16, from Q). Rather, the prescriptions of the Mosaic Law are assumed true and upheld. Thus, Jesus' command to the leper to go and show himself to the priest (Mk 1:44 = Mt 8:4; Lk 5:14; and cf. Lk 17:14) is based squarely on the prescriptions of Lv 13 and 14. Herod Antipas is rebuked by John the Baptist for his incestuous marriage (Mk 6:18 = Mt 14:4) in terms of the prohibitions of Lv 18:16 and 20:21. The owner of the vineyard in Jesus' parable, at the day's end, says to the foreman: "Call the workers and give them their pay," a directive in full accord with the requirement of Lv 19:13 (cf. Dt 24:15) that wages not be withheld overnight.

It is sometimes said that Christian teaching left the *ethical* precepts of the Law completely intact, except for prohibiting remarriage after divorce and abolishing the law of retribution. This is true. It is further said that all *legal and ceremonial* prescriptions lapsed in Christian practice, which is not true. Payment of the temple tax is one example of continuing observance (Mt 17:24; cf. Ex 30:13 and 38:26). Mention of the fringe on Jesus' garment required by Nm 15:37–39 is another (Mk 6:56 = Mt 9:20; 14:36; Lk 8:44). There is also private sacrifice (Mt 5:23) and sabbath-keeping (Mt 24:20). The code for church discipline contained in Mt 18:15–18 includes the requirement from Dt 19:15 that only on the evidence of two or three witnesses shall a charge be sustained.

Matthew's understanding of the Law does not differ in principle from that of the rabbis. The rabbinic principle after the founding of the academy at Iavneh turned out to be one of accommodation of the written precepts to new conditions. Matthew leaves the tradition of the Jewish scribal office intact. Jesus will send his community "prophets and wise men and scribes" (Mt 23:34). He praises "every scribe learned in the reign of God" (13:52). The evangelist maintains the rightness of practices such as almsgiving, prayer, and fasting (6:1–18), even swearing oaths if it is honestly done (23:20ff.; this contrasts with the rejection of oaths found in 5:33–37). Tithing is to continue (23:23). In the latter verse "justice, mercy and good faith" are called the "weightier matters of the Law." Yet Matthew employs a Q saying (23:23c = Lk 11:42) which insists: "It is these [weightier things] you should have practiced, without neglecting the others." In other words, nothing of the Law is to pass.

Matthew willingly grants to the scribes and Pharisees that they "have succeeded Moses as teachers" (Mt 23:2). Their teaching is not attacked but is declared to be binding. It is only their practice, when it is hypocritical, that is condemned (vv. 3f.).[8]

At times in Matthew the charge of perversion of the "commandment of God for the sake of your 'tradition' " (Mt 15:3) is so much to the fore that the legitimate function of the Pharisees' scribes seems to be forgotten (cf. 15:6, 9, 14; 16:6, 11). In these passages the tension between Matthew's allegiance to Jesus' words and the demands for adherence to the oral law (by some Christian Jews?) is evident. In the six antitheses between "the commandment imposed on the ancients" and Jesus' "But I say to you," Matthew's interpretation sharpens the Law by refining the meaning of murder, adultery, and a false oath (5:22–26, 28–30, 34–37). The refinement seems to be an abolition in the case of divorce and the law of retaliation (vv. 32, 39–42). The sixth case, "Love your countryman and hate your enemy" (v. 43), in part unbiblical, is likewise revoked. The popular tradition represented by the latter half of the phrase is found in the Rule of the Community of Qumrân.[9]

The one major command running through Matthew's gospel is that of mercy (cf. Mt 5:7; 9:13; 12:7; 18:33; 25:31–46). Joined to it is trust in Jesus' authority (cf. 8:10, 13; 9:2, 22, 28f.) and in his person (cf. 18:6; 27:42). This trust has the double sense in 23:23 of fidelity—to the tithing prescriptions of the Law (Lv 27:30)—and "the essence of the better righteousness by which discipleship of Jesus can be recognised."[10]

Justice or righteousness for Matthew is therefore the fruit of God's grace in Jesus Christ. This evangelist seeks the just character of Jews under the Law—both in Jesus' own time (Mt 1:19) and before (13:17; 23:29, 35). Moreover, it is something available in his day through right observance of the Law. The prophets, the just, and the lowly ("one of these least")—all "saints" under the Law—are to be received in Jesus' name (10:41f.). The justice of his disciples will link them with all the just of past ages who kept the Law. In this way they are united with the history of Israel and its promise, and separated from the "scribes and Pharisees," whose sin in Matthew's eyes is that they negate the Law by rationalizing it away.

One verse that causes Matthew difficulty is the advice to do "all" that the rabbis teach (Mt 23:3). This would include the whole oral law, the "tradition," as well as written Torah.[11] Yet Matthew counsels numerous departures from it. One clear case occurs in 15:20 (also 15:2) where we are told that Christians eat with unwashed hands and need not wash them. The washing of hands is not required because its protagonists are busy nullifying God's word (15:6). Yet Matthew does not set the whole tradition aside summarily, as Mark does (Mk 7:1–16). He has a new principle with which to interpret the Law: loving speech and thought prevail over observance (Mt 15:11, 18–20a). The scandal of the Pharisees is met head on (v. 12). They are not a "planting" of God, hence they will be uprooted (v. 13). Because their teaching is a way of blindness, they need not be followed (v. 14).

Failure in the Preaching Mission

In many ways Matthew is aware of rabbinic thought and prone to use its terms. Still he is severe on the subject of the judgment pronounced on Israel, the "sons of the kingdom" (Mt 8:11f.; cf. 21:43). Mark has Jesus speaking in parables to those outside "so that they may see but not perceive" (Mk 4:12, citing Is 6:9f.). Matthew changes this to *"because* seeing they do not see" (Mt 13:13). This terminology, with which the gospel abounds, shows the complete opposition between the Jewish Christians and the Jewish community in Matthean circles. (Persecution is attributed to fathers and brothers, flogging takes place "in your synagogues": 10:23; 23:34; the "whole people" is conscious of the meaning of Jesus' death: 27:25.)

Matthew assumes throughout his gospel that the message about Christ has been preached to the Jews in Palestine, who have refused it.[12] Jesus' instructions for the preaching mission (Mt 10:5f.) follow this sequence: the lost sheep of the house of Israel, not pagans or Samaritans; courts and synagogues; then rulers and kings. The passage ends with an expected rejection (10:17f.). Matthew's main interest, though, is not in the pre-resurrection preaching tour but in the failure of post-resurrection evangelism in Israel. This failure he considers preordained (13:11–15). God has not accepted Israel because it has not accepted his messiah (21:43; 22:7f.; 23:38). Matthew recalls the Jewish mission sadly, with its persecutions, floggings, and huntings down (10:23; 23:34). There remains but one mission now: to all the gentiles (28:19).

Eschatology and Law

Ernst Käsemann reconstructs a situation in which the earliest Palestinian communities gathered around charismatic figures who exercised prophecy as judgment. Their teaching expressed "declarations of holy law," by which Käsemann means prophetic admonitions as to how God would act on the last day if believers were unfaithful to their calling.[13] Thus Mt 7:2 (=Mk 4:24f.; eliminated from Lk 8:18) says that judgment on Christians will depend upon how they act on what they hear. At the conclusion of the Lord's prayer, God's eschatological forgiveness is tied to willingness to forgive (Mt 6:14f.). In Mt 5:19, to relax the least of the commandments and teach others to do so is to be judged least in the kingdom of heaven.

Käsemann's chief argument for the early character of these sentences—not authentic Jesus sayings but the first stratum of church sayings—is their recourse to the Son of man as universal judge expected soon.[14] He thinks they reflect that early time when enthusiasm was still abroad and there was as yet no administrative or disciplinary law in the church. That development was already on its way by the time Mark wrote his gospel. When Matthew was written, early Christian prophecy was so subordinated to good order in the community that the dictates of the early prophet-leaders had largely disappeared. In place of the earliest clear judgments, in which adverse divine sanction was assured for those who would not judge themselves now, the fragmentary relics cited above appear in the synoptic gospels. Some of them are already being modified from a prophetic to a hortatory character.

This much seems to be established: that in the primitive church, Spirit and Law were not separated. From the beginning the Spirit was viewed as the promulgator and ground of the Law, which was not understood as the individual prescriptions of Torah. The Spirit was the ensurer of obedience in a community that knew itself to be under judgment, naming reprobation as the high penalty of failure. This outlook was not unlike that of the terrible, swift sanctions of Bible times. Primitive fragments of this type of NT law led to developed church law. The latter is not to be deplored as a decline from the highest ideal, which is Käsemann's theory, nor is the introduction of exhortation synonymous with corruption. Only a nostalgic conception of the primitive church would suggest that, or one that viewed the law of love as having no connection with Mosaic Law. Such an outlook would be Marcionite. The law of Christ was a law of love because the Sinai dispensation had been a law of love. "God vindicates his righteousness on earth through the medium of his law. We must not therefore speak of a polarity between grace and law. Grace is the power of God which creates salvation and in such a way that God remains Lord and Judge and maintains law."[15] It is a basic tenet of nineteenth-century theological liberalism that in Christianity the Law was completely superseded by love. Whatever else may be said of this view, it is not one that squares with the NT data.

LUKE

Most scholars agree that with the writing of Luke-Acts the first-century church faced the fact that the Lord's return was not imminent. With that urgent expectation in recession, there set in a kind of accommodation to structures, which some describe as "early catholicism." Primitive Christianity in the image of Jesus as interpreted by Paul was in decline until the Reformers rediscovered its true meaning. Freedom from the Law is such an accomplished fact by Luke's time that he mentions law only as a past epoch within redemptive history. Conzelmann, Haenchen, and G. Barth associate themselves with this view.[16] Basic to it is the supposition that Luke's major if not sole concern is with gentile Christianity. But Franz Overbeck challenged this view a century ago; Adolf von Harnack did the same in his book on the Acts of the Apostles in 1908; and the Norwegian scholar Jacob Jervell in our own day has called Luke-Acts a work of gentile Christianity profoundly interested in Jewish Christianity.[17] Let us examine these assumptions.

Luke modifies the passage about "wars and rumors of wars" (Mk 13:7; Mt 24:6) to make it say that the "end will not be at once" (Lk 21:9) rather than "not yet." There will be famines and pestilences, terrors, and great signs from heaven, but "before all this" there will be persecution (v. 12), as if Luke were confident that some time would elapse before the Lord's return. The persecution of the community is not an infallible sign, in other words, that the end is near. Much is made of his change from, "But he who endures to the end will be saved" (Mk 13:13*b;* Mt 24:13), to, "By your endurance you will gain your lives" (Lk 21:19). The elimination of "the end" does not seem highly significant. Conzelmann stresses the notion that Luke looks to the present of the community, with a modest interest in a reign of God that lies in the future. This may be true, but the distinction is a subtle one. Luke's division of history into three epochs (cf. Lk 16:16; Lk 4:16–21 and Ac 10:38; Ac 1:11 and 2:38ff.), of which the present is the third, is an easier matter to discern.

Conviction about Luke's diminished interest in an imminent parousia as a motive for expectation and repentance has led to the supposition that he had more this-worldly ethical concerns than his predecessors. He features divine forgiveness, which leads him correspondingly to tell parables of the divine compassion. But he continues to have an eschatological concern quite like that of Mark and Matthew. He is simply prepared for a longer wait than they are. His concern for ethical living in the present does not prove to be greater than theirs, but neither is it less. Luke stresses the love commandment as the one that best interprets the Law through the story of the good Samaritan (Lk 10:27–29) or multiplied touches that speak of a human sympathy resembling the divine. Overall, Luke is a theologian of God's dealings with humanity, not primarily of interpersonal dealings within the human community. Even his descriptions in Acts of mutual support in the Jerusalem church have more to do with unity as a sign of the Spirit's presence than an ethical imperative.

Israel or "New Israel"?

Most scholars take it for granted that for Luke the church
(a word he does not use) is the "new Israel"—a term nowhere
found in the NT.[18] Even though Paul's epistles, the other two
synoptics, and Q already existed at the time of Luke's writing, definitive settlement on the place of gentiles in a Jewish
church cannot be presumed to have been made. His two
books represent a solution to the problem which is by no
means that of Paul. He admires Paul but does not know his
thought very well. There is a slight possibility that he rejects
it in favor of what to him is a better solution. The uncircumcised were somehow living with the circumcised as believers
in Jesus. Luke writes as if no satisfactory theological rationale
has been found and he means to provide one. The terms of
the admission of the gentiles into the Jewish community have
probably been faced by James and Hebrews as well as by
Mark and Matthew. All are wrestling with the problems of
election, law, and covenant (and, by implication, circumcision), as they have been complicated by admitting large
numbers of gentiles into the covenant community. It is gratuitous to suppose that by the time Luke writes, even in his
immediate area, a church "establishment" has come into
being. Like the others, he is attempting to describe what God
is doing in a scheme of coexistence that is already a fact. He
cannot be proposing an "official" church solution any more
than the others. He is an interpreter of God's mysterious
ways, as are the rest.

The Law of Moses

When Luke speaks of the Law he means the entire dispensation under which Jews—including some who believe in
Jesus—live. Jervell has assembled under seven headings a
partial list of Luke's words for the Law used in the two books.
Many are peculiar to Luke among the NT writers and in
some cases altogether unique. The tone is Hellenist Jewish
and may reflect living contact with conservative congregations. Luke often speaks of "Moses" when he means the Law

(Lk 5:14; 16:29, 31; 24:27; Ac 6:11; 15:1, 21; 21:21); elsewhere, "the law of Moses" (cf. Lk 2:22; 24:44; Ac 13:38; 15:
5; 28:23), a phrase found in only three NT passages outside
of Luke. Moses is "proclaimed in the synagogues" in Luke's
writings only (Ac 15:21), but also "spoken against," sometimes with "blasphemous utterances," as are the "ancestral
customs" (Ac 6:11, 13, 14 [18:13]; 15:1; 21:21, 28; 28:17).
Luke has Paul avow that he has never spoken against "the
law of the Jews" (Lk 25:8) and uses a Septuagintal word in
participial form for "violating the Law" (Ac 23:3), the only
time it occurs in the NT. Only he calls it "the law of the Lord"
(Lk 2:23, 24, 39) and the "ancestral law" (Ac 22:3). Finally,
what Moses received on Sinai to give to us were "living
words" (Ac 7:38). In none of the above cases does Luke have
anything in mind but the actual Law given through Moses to
Israel, the only Israel there is. He never understands by it
ethical precepts only. It includes the ceremonial in a way
that could easily take in the oral law ("the customs") also.

The narrative of Paul's nazirite vow certifies him as a true
Jew (Ac 21:15–26). Circumcision is always the real thing,
never figurative as in certain other NT passages (cf. Ac 15:1,
5; 16:3). "Uncircumcised in heart and ears" (Ac 7:51) is a
charge of failure to keep the whole Law. The primitive
church of Jerusalem is shown keeping the whole Law, including temple worship (cf. Ac 6–7), as Jesus' parents had done
(cf. Lk 2:21, 22, 24, 39). Peter adheres strictly to separation
from gentiles in Acts, even the God-fearer Cornelius (cf. Ac
10:13ff., 28; 11:3; the latter two verses reflect understandings
of the oral Law).

No Dot of the Law to Be Void

Nowhere in Luke's gospel does Jesus criticize the Law or
its individual prescriptions, not even by way of reinterpreta-
tion, as in Mark and Matthew. The charge of witnesses
against Stephen, who are described as "false," is that he
claimed "that Jesus the Nazorean will destroy this place [the
temple mount] and change the customs which Moses handed

down to us" (Ac 6:14). Nothing in Luke's gospel or in Acts
sustains the charge. The lengthy response of Stephen (Ac 7)
is meant to establish its falsehood. In Luke's gospel, Jesus
views the Law as permanently valid. There is no stress on
ethics that could give the impression that this part continues
in force while the ritual or cultic lapses.[19]

In support of this contention, note these data: Luke fails
to raise one commandment above the others, not even the
"law of love" (cf. Lk 10:25-28, where Luke changes Mark
to have the lawyer provide the answer, not Jesus); the omis-
sion of any repudiation of Moses in the teaching on divorce
or new interpretation by Jesus. (Cf. Lk 16:18, a saying
which, however interpreted, disturbs "no single stroke of a
letter of the Law," v. 17.) There is silence in Luke concerning kosher laws mentioned in Mk 7:1-23, even though Lk
11:38-44 indicates that that evangelist was familiar with the
Marcan material (cf. Ac 21:21-24; 28:17, where Paul is said
not to have contravened the "customs of the fathers").
Luke features almsgiving in the altered sayings of Lk 11:41
and 12:33; also Ac 10:2, 4, 31; 24:7. Finally, Luke-Acts insists that the Law's just demands be kept, even in sabbath
disputes (cf. Lk 13:16). In a word, Luke's Jerusalem community in Acts can be made up of "thousands of Jews who
have come to believe, all of them staunch defenders of the
Law" (Ac 21:20) only because in his gospel Jesus has never
so much as reinterpreted the Law, not to speak of changing
it.

This concept of an unalterable divine deliverance to Israel
is essential to the third evangelist. He never Christianizes the
Law or interprets it in a way to favor the church. He is the
great defender of Christians against charges of apostasy and
blasphemy. The Law is from God to Israel, not to anyone
else. It cannot be broken or ignored in the name of some
higher righteousness, not by Jesus, by Paul, or by gentile
believers who now think it their heritage in some sense.

First to the Jews

What is the meaning of Luke's absolute purism on this subject? Putting it down to a romantic or archaic spirit will not do. He has a clear theological purpose. For him Jew and gentile exist in the church side by side. Luke never makes Abraham the father of gentiles, always of the Jews, who are his offspring (cf. Lk 1:72–75; Ac 3:25f.; 7:8), in whom the nations of the earth are to be blessed. Luke is by no means without a theology of the participation of gentiles in the promise. His view is that of the Bible in seeing God's servant Jesus sent "to you [Jews] first" (Ac 3:26) in the spirit of a blessing to all through Abraham (cf. Gn 12:3) and David (cf. Ac 15:17; Am 9:11f.). The covenant of circumcision is extremely important to Luke. It affects salvation (cf. Lk 1:70ff.) and is not to be set aside by any subsequent settlement, least of all by the son of Zechariah.

Luke's Christian Jews accept all that is written in the Law and all that the prophets say about a "circumcised Messiah promised the people and now come."[20] He is much interested in those who will not be turned from their evil ways (cf. Ac 3:26). They have lost their inheritance, unlike Jewish believers in Jesus who have entered into it. The latter have circumcision and the Law as the badge of their membership in the church, so to say. Frequently Acts mentions their numbers, for Luke cannot see the providential plan as failing. Any gentile acceptance of Jesus not built on a Jewish nucleus is incomprehensible to him. Otherwise, how could the blessing of the nations *through* the seed of Abraham make any sense? Only in this way can the church be known for what it is.

Far from tolerating Christian Jewish observance of the Law, Luke demands it. The hut of David rebuilt by God from its ruins (cf. Ac 15:16), the restored Israel, is not a figurative matter but literal in the Christian Jewish community. The gentiles for their part are saved as gentiles (cf. Ac 10–11 and 15)—namely, as part of the salvation of Israel. The texts that make this especially clear occur in Simeon's song (Lk 2:30ff.), the utterances of Paul and Barnabas at Pisidian Antioch (Ac 13:26, 46f.) and Symeon Peter and James in Jerusalem (Ac 15: 7ff., 14). In the last verse, God is spoken of as having "first" concerned himself "to take from among the gentiles a people for his name," hence there are a people and an associate people. Luke is not devoid of Pauline language on faith as justifying both (cf. Ac 13:38f., 48*b;* 15:8f.). He even has statements redolent of Paul, such as that forgiveness of sins is being preached in Jesus, "including the remission of all those charges you could never be acquitted of under the Law of Moses" (Ac 13:38), and, "Why do you . . . try to place a burden on these [gentile] converts which neither we nor our fathers were able to bear?" (Ac 15:10). Here Luke transmits without comment a position of Christians and some rabbis on the Law. He adds also the more general comment—found throughout the Bible—that Israel always had trouble keeping the Law (cf. Ac 7:53). He cannot mean by this that in principle it is impossible to observe the Law; if he thought so, he would have omitted it as canceling out his other statements. His Christian Jews can and do observe the Law (cf. Ac 21:15–26). This is the only point of the judgment of James (later known as the "just," i.e., the Law observant) that gentiles were to be held to the lesser observance of the four precepts to which resident aliens were bound by Lv 17–18 (cf. Ac 15:20, 28–29*a*). Moreover, Paul and Barnabas urge the "Jews and God-fearing proselytes" to "persevere in the grace of God" (Ac 13:43). Undoubtedly life under the Law is a life of grace for Luke. This fact is not canceled out by the greater grace which he thinks has come to Jews and gentiles alike in Christ (cf. Lk 24:47; Ac 2:38; 4:12; 15:11).

At no point does Luke make a case for justification by the Law. When he says that "in him [Christ], everyone who believes is acquitted of everything for which there is no acquittal under the Law of Moses" (Ac 13:38f.), he does not contrast this with adherence to the Law. There is a vagueness here on how salvation in Christ is accomplished for observant Jews. Yet it is clear that no tradition that Luke may possess on the need of saving faith for all is going to interfere with his basic ecclesiological principle. The church is made up of adherents to the full Mosaic deliverance and of gentiles held to much less; both are saved by faith in the risen Christ. Without the former reality the charges that Luke has heard leveled against Paul in the diaspora would be true. But if Christian Jews do not keep the Law, then other Jews could accuse them of infidelity to a covenant delivered by a faithful God. Both before and after the Lucan settlement of Ac 15, Christian Jews keep the full Law. Luke cannot see it as "abrogated, replaced, or conceived as an epoch."[21]

It has been argued against Jervell and Nils A. Dahl, his mentor in these matters, that Luke's "account of the motivations of the gentile mission is neither logical nor theological."[22] Since, "at the time Luke wrote, it is generally agreed that Jewish Christianity was largely a spent force," we have in Acts an inconsistent theological solution to what is no longer a practical problem.[23] Christians, largely gentile, and Jews are the opposing partners in the polemic of Luke's day. His attempt to explain the origins of the gentile influx into the church is to "be judged historically worthless" but may be in part "a defence of the legitimacy of the Gentile Churches in the form of a defence of their co-founders [the apostles and Paul]."[24] S. G. Wilson, whose views these are, is familiar with Jervell's position that "with the conclusion of Acts there is also the conclusion of the mission to the Jews"; that unlike Paul, who envisions future Jewish belief in Jesus (in Rom 9–11), Luke excludes the possibility because "judgment by and on the Jews has irrevocably been passed."[25]

While this finality is doubtful on Jervell's own terms—"the Jews" being a people of whom myriads have believed in Jesus in the past (Ac 21:20), hence may well again—Wilson and Jervell are undoubtedly right in seeing no contemplated representation of the gospel to the Jews at the conclusion of Acts. Yet in Jervell's article on the Law in Luke-Acts, Luke's presentation there disclosed is so careful that his theological innocence or randomness can scarcely stand. The Christian

Jew is just as important to him as the non-Christian Jew. Even though the latter's numbers may be appreciably fewer at the time of the writing, the theological force of Luke's careful argument does not by that fact abruptly outlive its usefulness. It survives as an authentic theme of the NT for perpetual reflection by Christians.

THE SYNOPTIC TRADITION

In theological discussions of these matters, the underlying assumption usually is that Jewish practice is wrong, even for Jews. Christians have little ease in discussing the period in their own church before the final settlement, which they take to be Paul's. Whether a given practice was biblical or rabbinic, they take a kind of comfort in knowing that both were fated to pass from the Christian community. The thought of Jesus as an observant Jew is quickly dismissed, for if it was not Jesus from whom Paul got his principle of complete liberty from the Law (as his principle is thought to be), whence did he derive it? The paradox of a Master more committed to specific commands than his disciple, even in practice, is more than most Christians can bear.

We have not assumed that we have in the synoptic gospels any clear testimony to the practice of Christian Jews, either before the fall of Jerusalem or after. From the sources, the practice is ambiguous. Moreover, these believers are more aptly called Jewish Christians by the time the synoptics are written. Mark, Matthew, and Luke were all written for mixed communities of Jewish and gentile Christians in which the latter dominated, at least culturally. Mark was composed possibly for gentiles only, without special reference to keeping the Law. In its stress on the controversies in which Jesus engaged with the Pharisees, Mark gives the impression that to follow Jesus as a disciple is to be totally free in one's legal interpretation as Jesus was. Mark's Jesus brings salvation as the fulfillment of apocalyptic history in the manner of Daniel

and the Books of Enoch and Jubilees but without their fullness of imagery. This evangelist possesses traditions about
Jesus' discussions of the Law (cf. Mk 3:5; 7:13*b*, 19*b*) but
presents them only to reinforce Jesus' sovereign role as
inaugurator of the end-time.

Matthew and Luke are both concerned with the way in
which Jesus fulfills the history of the Jewish people, which to
them is incomprehensible apart from the Law. Both engage
in redactional activity of their sources. Retaining some historical substrate of Jesus' teaching, they fashion it in two directions: Matthew to show that Jesus is the authentic teacher of
the Law whose interpretation must be followed in preference to others that are current; Luke to establish that the
pious remnant of Jews from which Jesus sprang led organically to a Jewish minority of believers in him, while the majority refused to accept the gospel. Neither Matthew nor
Luke can be thought of as protagonists of Christian Jewishness—rather, the opposite. Yet their traditional materials
convince them that Jesus is the bearer of salvation in essential continuity with what has gone before.

Robert Banks's *Jesus and the Law in the Synoptic Tradition* brings up to date the voluminous literature on this subject. His method is one of presenting the teaching of Jesus on
the Law in the gospels from which community creations and
evangelists' redactions can be "subtracted."[26] Such confidence in possessing the core of Jesus' sayings as it existed
before the editing process in the early church began has not
marked the discussion in this chapter. Banks is convinced
that Jesus' obedience to the mission he had been called to was
his primary concern and that a negative attitude to the oral
tradition surrounding the Law was merely a by-product of
this. He dismisses the view of Windisch, Branscomb, and
others that Jesus did not repudiate the oral law as a whole.
He holds that gospel indications about Jesus' speaking blessings over food, singing the Passover Hallel, and wearing the
customary Jewish robe had nothing to do with the oral tradition but could be traced to ordinary religious practice of the

times. Neither did Jesus actively provoke the Pharisees over
the sabbath and defilement. He simply went about his mission directed from within. As a result of this, conflicts followed. As to the Law itself, even though Banks adverts to the
passages where Jesus is reported as supporting it (e.g., Mt 5:
17–19; 22:37–40; 23:3), his exegesis leads him to conclude
that the more radical demands of Jesus' teaching "at every
point . . . transcend and surpass the demands of the Law."[27]
Matthew's christological emphasis everywhere takes precedence over matters such as righteousness, perfection, and
the love command.

The notion of the radical demands of Jesus' teaching is a
fairly standard Christian finding. It raises the question: Transcend and surpass *what* "demands of the Law"—those of the
postexilic redactors of the Mosaic books, or Jesus' rabbinic
contemporaries, or the emerging academy of Iavneh? It is
quite in order to hold that Jesus made a difference and that
the evangelists recorded the difference they thought Jesus
made. This is not the same as holding that Jesus so sove-
reignly transcended the Law that all gospel reference to it is
but background to the gospels' primarily kerygmatic purpose concerning him. In each gospel, Banks holds, Jesus'
"fundamental position with regard to it [the Law] is accu-
rately reflected."[28] A footnote at this point concurs with the
view of Martin Werner of 1923 that in each gospel, although
under a different form, the presupposition of the Pauline
understanding of the Law may be found.

GOD'S PERFECT LAW

While Banks does not fall into the usual trap of finding the
Jesus of the synoptics distinguishing between the moral and
the ceremonial demands of the Law ("no fundamental de-
marcation was made"),[29] his conclusions seem to flow from
the evidence of the gospels less certainly than those of an
older contemporary, John Knox.[30] In an insightful essay

largely unencumbered by the appartus of scholarship, Knox points out that the church, in accepting the Hebrew Bible as inspired, never let NT teaching stand alone. "The New Testament ethic has its roots in prophetism and Pharisaism," he writes, "and, in its true mind, the church has never thought of denying that connection."[31] If the biblical tradition is one in which the commandments can be kept, the NT adds, in the spirit of Jesus' teaching, God's perfect Law which cannot be fully kept. "The New Testament was added to the Old; not the Old to the New."[32]

The fact of the impossibility, in Knox's view, should not lead to frustration, despair, or a flight from the imperative force of Jesus' teaching. A certain way of understanding and emphasizing the grace of God and the freedom it confers will always be a temptation, but "a reaction against legalism issues in a virtual antinomianism."[33]

Jesus multiplied ethical demands in the synoptic gospels by specifying what the Law—a law of love—required. Yet he said that his yoke was smooth and his burden light, that he did not impose heavy and insupportable burdens. He did not speak of what God was doing through him as "justifying" (a legal term) but, especially in Luke's parables, as forgiving. In the community of grace which his followers would make up, there would be forgiveness. The point is not that Jesus gives a command to be perfect, impossible of fulfillment, and then says that the Father stands ready to forgive the inevitable failure. It is, rather, that to be human is necessarily to stand under God's ethical demand. Jesus tells what this demand is: no less than godlike perfection. One recalls the biblical command, "Be holy even as I am holy." A human community will fall short of the divine ideal in any case. In Jesus' teaching, his followers have the assurance that repentance and forgiveness are available, because the Father is a God of love.

Jesus in the synoptic gospels requires the recognition of obligation and earnest effort to discharge it. The God he preaches offers not only forgiveness but the highest kind of righteousness. Both are God's gift and not a human achievement. The God of Jesus does not "love" us, as in Paul. We are to love him and love our neighbor. He imposes on us categorical demands. Without saying that ritual or cultic behavior is no longer important, we must say that Jesus in the synoptics addresses us with utmost moral seriousness. The realm of grace he envisions is one in which the believer continues to be under obligation to God, called to the highest possible goodness, not released from it. To achieve this goodness, no measure of obedience to rules or principles will do. One has to will to forgive seventy times seven times. The desire will do for the deed. To follow Jesus in obedience to God's command is to forgive others and be assured of forgiveness from him in return. It is to achieve true goodness, which will inevitably be God's creation more than humanity's achievement.

SUMMARY

In conclusion, it appears that the following essentials of Christian faith are found in the synoptic gospels:

—The world and all that is in it is good. Only sin, the rebellious choice of creatures against the will of God, is evil, while catastrophes apart from sin go to make up a God-sent "test" or "trial."

—Humanity has been empowered by God to choose freely in response to his commands. Jesus shares this conviction with all the Jews who went before him.

—Mysterious forces which escape human control, known to the evangelists as "unclean spirits" or "demons," either have a separate existence or are lodged deep in the human psyche. Whichever the case, they are not to be feared, since trust in God through Jesus can overcome them. The power of such forces is as nothing compared to the holiness of God.

—No theory of the origins of sin is espoused by the evangelists or Jesus. It is taken as a tragic fact of human life and one that is presumably as old as the human race.

—God is gracious toward humanity, has always been, and ever will be. The grace he first showed in creation he continued to show to Israel through covenant and Law, a graciousness he cannot be thought of as interrupting but only continuing with the teaching of his "son" Jesus.

—The wonder-working career and teaching of the meaning of the Law by Jesus is the inauguration of the "final age." This career has about it the character of salvation that marked God's action in the time of the patriarchs and the prophets, Moses and Elijah in particular.

—Loving God and fellow countryman takes the form of obedience to God's will. It is the proper response to his call to enter into his "reign."

—The Law given through Moses must be kept by all, Jew and gentile alike. Jesus was the one dependable teacher who taught how.

—The way that gentiles are to keep the Law is taught differently by different synoptic evangelists. How Jews in the evangelists' churches are keeping the Law they do not tell us; nor do they express any thoughts on what continuing observance of the Law in the Jewish community may be accomplishing. Their main concern in this area is with Jews who actively resist faith in Jesus.

—The Law continues in force as an ordinance of God for the synoptics. They cannot conceive of a community called Israel, believing in Jesus, that it does not bind.

Chapter III

IS CHRIST THE END
OF THE LAW?

Paul's treatment of grace and law is central to this book, for it is his position—widely thought to be an opposition between faith in Jesus Christ and the dead works of the Law—that has prevailed in Christian thought. The question is, does such a summary fairly represent his teaching? In what sense does he hold that "Christ is the end of the Law"? This chapter will deal with these questions. It will also try to say whether Paul's anticipation of Christ's return so relativized all earthly reality that Christians have been bound to hold it in contempt ever since.

Correspondence by the apostle Paul to his churches was occasional in nature. No authentic letter can be taken as a theological treatise. All were written to cope with problems that had arisen in the various communities. The epistle to the Romans, whose city he had not yet visited, was perhaps a rationale for Jews and gentiles new in Christ on living at peace with one another. It was, in any case, a defense of Paul's gospel for those who may have heard adverse reports about it.

Romans was the most influential statement ever to have been made by a follower of Jesus on the subject of grace and law. Paul had looked into the problem in some detail as early as A.D. 54–55 in his letter to the Galatians. Subsequently, in the Corinthian correspondence (55–56) and in his letter to Philippi (which may be dated as early as 56 or as late as 62) the subject was further discussed. The Protestant reform of the sixteenth century can claim as its proudest achievement the restoration to Christian consciousness of the central place that God's graciousness in Christ had in Paul's thought. For him, the outstanding feature of God's gift was the inauguration of a new eon in which the Law, with its claim against the human race, yielded to divine forgiveness. When God declared, and in fact made, that race "just" without the necessity of continued observance of the Law as a condition, reconciliation occurred.

This teaching has a troubled history. The preaching of God's reign in the ministry of Jesus, as the gospels testify to it, does not view the Law as totally expendable (which seems to be Paul's position). Moreover, the opposite of "life in Christ" for Paul appears to be Judaism: not the Jewish people, but Judaism. This seeming opposition found its way into the heart of the Christian reform movement in Europe four centuries ago because of the central place the Reformers gave to Paul's teaching on justification. This brought even further suffering upon Jews, who had already endured quite enough at the hands of Christians.

WHO WERE THE JEWS THAT TROUBLED PAUL?

Paul, the Jew of Tarsus, doubtless brought the wrath of fellow Jews on his own head with the penning of his Galatian letter, but the tension had begun with 1 Thessalonians. This first letter from Paul had charged that the Jews "killed both the Lord Jesus and the prophets, and drove us out. . . . [They] displease God and oppose all men by hindering us from speaking to the gentiles that they may be saved" (1 Thes 2: 15–16a). Disputed on internal critical but not on textual grounds, this passage testifies to Paul's personal experiences with the fellow-circumcised. It probably refers to the Jews of Judea exclusively. The term "the Jews," who were troubling the Christians in Thessalonica, is set in contrast with "your own countrymen" (v. 14), the Thessalonians. This suggests

that Judean Christians were being persecuted by their Jewish kinsmen, not by Jews in general. Indeed, throughout
Paul's letters the terms "Jews," those who "keep the Law,"
and "the circumcision" consistently refer to others than the
Jews who are "in Christ," which would include himself and
his converts.

This language, reinforced by the vocabulary of the fourth
gospel, has provided Jews generally with much pain over the
centuries. They are the circumcised who keep the Law of
Moses. Judaism is their religion. The ethnic Jew who is a
Christian belongs to a company so small as to be negligible,
while Christians are almost universally of non-Jewish stock.
As a result the false supposition has spread that Paul's primary concern was with those who were ethnic Jews and their
opposite numbers who were not, the gentiles. Paul's believers and non-believers in Jesus, however, cut across those
blood lines completely.

To rely upon law as having saving power apart from faith
—not the Mosaic Law, but any religious stipulation—is a state
of mind. It is a gentile phenomenon as much as a Jewish one.
The precise reason for God's reprobation of the pagans, as
Paul spelled it out in Rom 1, was that they knew God's decree
in their hearts, yet committed every foolish perversion of it
(v. 32). Similarly, there were Jews who knew the Mosaic Law
and yet sinned against it in the grossest ways (Rom 2:17–24).
Paul speaks of the gentiles who, not having the Law,
nonetheless keep it as by instinct (Rom 2:14). He does not
refer to pagans who rely on their instinctive fulfillment of
prescribed religious practice to save them. We do not know
whether he encountered any, but we may presume it since
the mentality is everywhere. We can be sure that his adverse
judgment on such persons would be the same as on compla-
cent Christians or Jews.

Paul's starting point was the hearers of his gospel—Jews
and gentiles alike—who either accepted it or did not. He
generalized freely on these living contemporaries. He likewise generalized on the sinful condition of all humanity that

had lived from Adam to Christ. Paul did not express a view on the future condition of those Jews and gentiles alike who would never hear the gospel. Of them, he had nothing to say. He expressed no opinion on the Jews of future ages born into a culture that would view obedience to the Law as saving because it was of God. Jews who would in practice never be faced with the gospel as a way to live Jewish lives—that is, most of the Jews who have ever lived on the earth—are not considered in his letters.

The church, however, has been vocal where Paul was silent. It has derived from Paul's reflections on the small number who went unmoved by his preaching in his lifetime a confident view of God's judgment upon all Jews for all time. The logic is faulty, of course. At its root is this important question: Could Paul have been as certain as he seemed to be that his Jewish contemporaries had resisted his teaching about Christ in the spirit of his accusation? If that assumption is unfounded, then the logic of much of his argument falls to the ground.

PAUL'S CENTRAL MESSAGE

The central message of Paul is not by any means that the Jewish people are repudiated or their covenant abrogated with the death and resurrection of Jesus Christ. His central message is that Christ's obedient death and glorious vindication are God's gift to all humanity, inaugurating the new age for which the Jews had long hoped, and improving the lot of non-Jews identically with that of Jews. Paul's theme, as a disciple of his puts it, is that God has acquired a people made up of Jews and gentiles "for the praise of his glory" (Eph 1: 14; cf. v. 6). There exists a new and mysterious reality, the church, of which Christ is the head, even as he is the chief figure in the cosmos (Col 1:18). This church is a marvel of human unity and reconciliation (v. 20). It is not equivalent to the days of the Messiah, but exists as a pledge of the final age.

God's grace is available to all through membership in this community. The gift of God is justice through faith in Jesus Christ (Rom 1:17). Acceptance of the gift in faith has as its sign baptism into the death and resurrection of Christ (Gal 3:23–27; Rom 6:3–5).

CAN THE LAW BE KEPT?

The major question to be explored is whether Paul's teaching on the grace of Christ obliterates all guidance provided by law, be it of Sinai or inborn nature. He says, "If you are guided by the spirit, you are not under the law" (Gal 5:18). And again, "The whole law has found its fulfillment in this one saying: 'You shall love your neighbor as yourself' " (v. 14). The "law of Christ" will be fulfilled by the Galatians if they carry one another's burdens (6:2). The epistle to the Romans says to that church: "You are now under grace, not under the law" (Rom 6:14), and, "You died to the law through the body of Christ" (7:4).

The Law is praised as something "of the spirit," however, in contrast to "weak flesh" (Rom 7:14). It is likewise "holy," even as "the command" is "holy and just and good" (v. 12). Despite this admission, which is one that any pious Jew should make, "all who depend on works of the law [as contrasted with all who believe with the faith of Abraham] are under a curse" (Gal 3:10). To rely on the Law to save (lit., "whoever are of the works of the Law") is evidently the flaw in Paul's eyes. In his boldest of rabbinic transpositions, he quotes Dt 27:26, "Cursed be anyone who fails to fulfill all the provisions of this law." "All" occurs in the Septuagint—which Paul is not quoting exactly—but not in the Masoretic text in Hebrew. He thereby places under a curse observant Jews who fail in any particular, as he intimates they must. Elsewhere, however, he suggests with equanimity that he himself has been a perfect observant (see Gal 1:14; Phil 3:6*b*).

Still Paul affirms that sin is universal and prevents all from perfectly doing God's will. "All have sinned and all are deprived of the glory of God" (Rom 3:23). Such a statement is preliminary to Paul's declaration that all are justified "gratuitously by God's grace through redemption in Christ Jesus" (v. 24). Clearly the latter universality governs the former. A gift held out to all corresponds to the needs of all. Paul means it when he says all members of the human race are sinners. All need redemption if they are to be made right with God, that is, justified or given title to his glory. Jews and Greeks alike are "under [the domination of] sin" (v. 9). Paul states rhetorically, using the first person for emphasis, that "no good dwells in me, that is, in my flesh" (7:18). He attributes powerlessness to the Law "in that it was weakened through flesh" (8:3). "Those who are in the flesh [i.e., live as if in the former eon] cannot please God" (v. 8).

The catalog seems complete. "Sin" is the condition of active alienation from God. "Flesh" is the rebellious nature that confirms this condition. "Grace" is the opposite condition to sin, reversing the trend toward disobedience and destruction. God sent his son in the likeness of sinful flesh "as a sin offering, thereby condemning sin in the flesh, so that the just demands of the Law might be fulfilled in us who live, not according to the flesh, but in the spirit" (8:3f.).

The Pauline antithesis between law and grace, flesh and spirit, sin and redemption is worked out as a cosmic drama in which God proposes and man or the forces of evil dispose. Life is offered but death is chosen. The human condition is self-inflicted. Even though sin is personified, that is, described as something active in itself and different from the sum total of sins, it is nonetheless the result of human choice. It is willful on humanity's part, just as grace, its diametric opposite, is something willed on God's part. Grace must be accepted in faith if the human race is to possess it and be once again in friendship with the God who made it.

JUSTICE AND JUSTIFICATION

We have been using the words "justice" and "justification" without defining them. In Paul the noun is *dikaiosynē*, translated by each of the words above and "righteousness" as well. In three main passages (1 Cor 1:30; 2 Cor 5:21; Phil 3:9) the term is best taken ethically: God's justness or righteousness become ours in Christ. Basic to this concept is the corporate-Christ idea found in Paul. Christ is seen as an exclusive figure. All else than he is not-he. To believe is to be "in Christ." The concept is "both personal, because it requires personal faith and relation to Christ, and also corporate, because there is a new unity of mankind in him."[1] A solidarity of life and righteousness contrasts with a solidarity of sin and death in Adam (cf. Rom 5:12–21; 1 Cor 15:22). This new unity in Christ makes the church his body (cf. 1 Cor 12:12); it involves dying and rising with him (cf. Col 3:1–17; Rom 6:2, 11f.; Eph 4: 17–24); it constitutes believers a new creature or creation (cf. 2 Cor 5:17; Gal 6:15). This new life and all that goes with it is future but is entered into now (cf. 1 Cor 15:20ff.; Rom 6: 4, 6; 7:4). The incorporative notion includes redemption and the subsequent life of the redeemed. Christ is the place where salvation occurs. To be in him is to be renewed morally, i.e., with the power of a new life, and to be in a publicly known condition. The individual is in the Lord and the whole Christ is in each expression of his corporate personality.

By virtue of this incorporation, ethical justice becomes the possession of the one thus incorporated. In Christ we become the "justice of God" (2 Cor 5:21). Christ Jesus is "our wisdom, our justice, our sanctification, and our redemption" (1 Cor 1: 30). The justice that Paul possesses comes through faith in Christ, which is the power flowing from his resurrection (cf. Phil 3:9f.). When Paul exhorts and commands, that language often implies an indicative as well as the expressed imperative: the Christian already is in an ethical state of justice.

Besides this ethical conception of justice, Paul also has a doctrine of justification by faith (Rom 5:1; Gal 2:16) from which the possibility of righteous conduct flows. God's grace is the sole agent by which the believer is accepted, acquitted, forgiven. In Bultmann's term, anglicized from the German, he is "rightwised." The believer is made just or righteous by God's activity, becoming thereby a new kind of person. In sharing in the risen life of Christ the believer acquires new ethical power, but the fundamental righteousness remains Christ's. Christ shares it by living in the believer (see Gal 2: 20), and this sharing is the believer's justification.

Justification in Christ "spells the end of law-justification,"[2] understood as law fulfillment by human effort. God looks on people as they are found in Christ and sees nothing but his own justice there. Paul demands righteousness of believers (cf. Rom 6:19), but as in Mt 5 he sees it as a gift as well. It is inseparable from the Giver, who is God in Christ. The gift is something in which the believer lives. It is never his own, however much the fruits of his justice "which Jesus Christ has ripened in you" (Phil 1:11) may seem to be his. Jesus, whose justice received from God is concentrated in his self-giving on the cross (Rom 5:18f.), is the new inclusive Man. His justice is intended to be that of others.

The link in Paul between God's justifying of humanity, viz., his declaring it right with him, and his sharing of Christ's own righteousness with believers is the apostle's use of a verb and nouns from the same root. There is hence no real question of an "imputing" or an "imparting," in terms of the classical Protestant-Catholic debate. There is a Pauline doctrine in which a double affirmation is made: namely, that by faith the individual receives *justification* (God's deed), and also by faith possesses *justice* or *righteousness* (a human reality resulting from incorporation into Christ). The two are inseparable, even though "justification" does not mean "making ethically righteous." Justification is a state. In that state, the ethical fruits of Christ's righteousness are reaped.

PAUL'S VIEW OF CREATION

This discussion of words and concepts essential to Paul's presentation of law and grace sends us back to basic questions. What was his view of the world—what we nowadays call "nature"—and the human creature? He does not tell us in so many words. Presumably, like any Jew, he viewed a cosmos that was good from the very fact that God made it. Yet he has no theme of a cosmic order such as the psalmists hymned or as found in Luke's Areopagus discourse attributed to him (cf. Ac 17:24–28). His descriptions of orderliness are confined to discussions of the duties of men as citizens, women, and slaves. He has no philosophical vision of true and universal order, only one of restored peace and creatureliness in the final age. Then and only then, with the restoration that is salvation, will humanity regain its true image. Unlike other Jewish thinkers of the time (insofar as their views are known), Paul did not suppose that a likeness to God has been retained by sinful humanity. For him, only Christ has and is that likeness. We cannot know the measure of the divine likeness that Paul would have ascribed to Adam before his sin, except to say that it was greater than after his sin. The only firm theological data we have from Paul are those on Christ.

It has been said that Paul is so interested in redemptive salvation that he has no interest in the creation. We know that he cares passionately about the human race and has thoughts on the future restoration of the cosmos. We are not at all informed on his view of the initial constitution of things. Bultmann has been criticized for his soteriological interpretation of Gal 4:4f. as insufficiently alert to Christ the mediator of creation.[3] Obviously Paul is speaking in that passage of deliverance from a condition of servitude under the Law—which he compares with minor age (v. 3)—to one of sonship of God. The "fullness of time" in v. 4 connotes some sort of preexistence of God's son whom he "sends." The same power operative in the redemption for Paul was operative in the creation, a fact that Bultmann seems to overlook. The apocalyptic categories implied by the terms Wisdom, Son of Man, and Kingdom provided a metaphysics of transcendence that preceded and include the creation. They were not a new stage in Paul's thought applicable only to the redemption of the human race in Christ.

Paul voices a doxology to God the Father and Christ, whom he calls Lord, by saying that it is through the latter that all things are, and we through him (1 Cor 8:6). A frustrated creation lives in hope because of the predestination of many to "share the image of his son" (Rom 8:18–21, 24, 29). This is taken to be an expression of Paul's total cosmic concern, not one that touches on human salvation only.

J. G. Gibbs emphasizes the importance for Paul of the relationship between Christ and the creation, "particularly since that cosmic work is congruent with Paul's other affirmations of Christ's sovereignty."[4] Pauline theology *begins* with the lordship of Jesus, "with the result that it sees the relation between the creation and the redemption"[5] as dynamic. Christ's lordship no less than God's ultimate dominion spans both. There can be "no creationless redemption (Rom 8:18ff.) and ultimately no redemptionless creation (Eph 1:10; Col 1: 20; etc.)."[6]

Paul's differences with the rabbis of the Tannaitic period (A.D. 1–200) were fundamental. This is so in part because there is no rationale in rabbinic sources on salvation and how it works comparable to that supplied by Paul in his letters. This much can be said: the rabbis had a general principle that to be Jewish was to have a share in the world to come. To doubt this proposition, as the Sadducees were said to do, could result in losing that share, as could disobedience to the Law for which there had been neither repentance nor forgiveness. Various opinions were put forward as to how gentiles could be saved. Paul's starting point was diametrically opposite. He thought that since all were under sin, Jews and

gentiles alike (cf. Gal 4:3ff.; Rom 3:9), all needed release from
the condition of enslavement.

The entire human predicament was graver for Paul than
for the rabbis. It was not a matter, as in Judaism, of sharing
in the world to come as a Jew (or proselyte or gentile) if one
kept the commandments and gained forgiveness for those
transgressed. Rather, one was lost without reconciliation to
God by faith acceptance of salvation in Christ. Paul does not
indicate how he came to think that all humanity was in such
a plight when apparently the rabbis thought otherwise. He
does not tell us whether he thinks that Adam's sin neces-
sitated deliverance from a condition of sin for individuals (cf.
Rom 5:12–19; 1 Cor 15:22) or that successive confirmation of
Adam's sin by individuals brought about the enslavement of
all (cf. Rom 5:12). In other words, there is no clear doctrine
of original sin in Paul as it was later understood—namely, a
condition of alienation of the individual from God at birth
before any personal sins had been committed. There is only
a universal condition of sin in Adam marking the old era and
a potentially universal one of grace in Christ marking the
new.

DISCONTINUITY IN HISTORY

Paul's universe is one of warring powers in the religious
sphere. Grace can make mutual service a possibility, but
outside of that healing influence—whether the other sphere
be Mosaic Law, pagan wisdom, or spirit-filled enthusiasm—
chaos prevails. Even in the light of the organic body of faith
which Paul envisions, where in mutual support members do
their part for the whole body, "the notion of an inherent
community of life is alien to Paul's thinking."[7] God's fidelity
is expressed in a series of remarkable inbreakings on human
history rather than anything continuous. The initial creation
is followed by redemption from destruction by the flood,
then the promise of grace, exodus, prophecy, and finally the

cross and resurrection. History for Paul is a record of God's successive challenges. The centuries do not flow smoothly into one another, nor does the human family proceed on its way unchanged. There are great disjunctions, one age displacing another. Thus, the epochs of Adam, Abraham, Moses, and Christ are sharply distinguished.

In similar fashion, the transfigured body that rises from the dead (1 Cor 15:35–49) is not the heavenly transformation of an earthly body in ordered succession. It will be new, "bearing the likeness of the man from heaven" (v. 49), Christ in his glorified state. There intervenes between the two stages a condition of nakedness. The natural body has been left behind, the spiritual one has not yet supervened. Then comes a "heavenly dwelling," which "envelops" us, "so that what is mortal may be absorbed by life" (2 Cor 5:2–5). The present situation of believers is one of lowliness and obedience. The power of the resurrection will shatter this earthly vessel. Discontinuity is thus the distinguishing feature of Paul's view of both existence and history.

How did Paul come to hold such opinions? They are unlike those of any Jewish near-contemporary, such as Hillel. Is Paul in any sense a man of the Bible? All attempts to discover exact parallels in either rabbinic thought or the philosophy and mystery religions of the diaspora have ended in failure. Jews understandably deplore Paul's departure from the Pharisee posture of his youth (cf. Phil 3:5), an appreciation of the Law which flowered in the rabbis. The history-of-religions school feels secure in ascribing pre-gnosis to him if not infection by Gnosticism itself, coupled with elements of "the Kyrios-cult and the sacraments [of] pre-Pauline Hellenistic Christianity."[8] Yet none of these accounts for his unique way of looking at the biblical data. The apocalyptic mentality of the Hellenist period was vigorous in Jewish circles and was not confined to the diaspora. However extensive Paul's early career in Palestine, if indeed he had one (cf. Ac 22:3), he could easily have been affected by the prevailing eschatologism even there. It was all-pervasive and subsided only slowly during the Tannaitic period. We do not find anything unique in Paul's idea of eons, nor in his supposition that by God's intervention the present age will yield to something more enduring. That much at least was common teaching.

Only in his total revitalizing of all Jewish and world history by a Christ standard do we find Paul characteristically un-Jewish. To account for this, the uniqueness of his experience of the resurrected Jesus would suffice. No search for parallels or cultural influences is necessary to explain the main shift in his thought categories. The unexpected and unrepeated would sufficiently account for that. The resurrection of Christ is not to be thought of as a key to all locks, as it sometimes is in Christian theology.

This relativization takes a particular form in the mind of this Jewish thinker who was already at home with "this age" and "the age to come." Speculation that we know was abroad at the time about the end of history stirred new imagination of its beginnings. In these we may have an immediate clue to the two races or "generations" toward which Paul gravitated.[9] His preference for Abraham over Moses would have been quite uncharacteristic of anyone committed in youth to the oral Law. Yet this could be accounted for by his skirmishes with protagonists of the Law such as he himself had been. Paul's silence on the figures of Enoch and Noah, both typologically popular in his day, is surprising. Had he wished to go from earliest beginnings to the Sinai revelation made to Moses, the rabbinic legend of the Noachian precepts or the Enoch speculations on "the son of man" would have provided interference for this sweeping purpose. Rather, he chose Abraham, a familiar Jewish figure, as the father of both Israelites and proselytes, and one whose trust that God would send his barren wife a son was proverbial. Better than anyone, he could bridge covenantal history from Adam to Moses. Paul needed someone who typified faith in a promise, not fulfillment of precepts.

IMPORTANCE OF THE INDIVIDUAL

Paul assigned a greater importance to the individual than did any other NT writer. He recorded many intimate friendships in his letters by way of greetings, and in general brought the person, whether believer or unbeliever, into prominence. It is important to observe that his soliloquy on rightdoing in Rom 7 is probably not autobiographical, his "inmost self" (v. 22) being a rhetorical construct. Also, his personalism is not of the modern sort that can sustain Bultmann in his concept of "authentic existence." Despite the eschatological dimension of many of Paul's ideas (e.g., that of detachment, living "as if not"), he remains an apostle of individual as well as of corporate existence.

A person is seldom a "soul" or "spirit" for Paul in the Greek manner (1 Cor 2:11 is an exception, reflecting the Stoic or popular philosophical view). Indeed, the words "flesh" (2 Cor 7:5) and "spirit" (2 Cor 2:13) are interchangeable for him to describe his own person. Even when he writes of "the spirit of the man that is in him" he is courting popular understanding by using an analogy for his greater concern: the divine spirit expressed in marvelous inbreakings on human life.

The apostle does not deny human gifts and capabilities, even when he stresses human "weakness." Actually he is not much interested in personal shortcomings, weaknesses, or even guilt. Just as "strength" comes from outside the individual—namely, from God—so "weakness" is induced by temptation from without. Far from seeing humanity as inherently powerless, Paul has a relatively robust view of its capacities. It is, however, the battleground of a cosmic struggle. It may trust in itself—which would be a yielding to idolatry—or rely on God. The claim of "strength" is rejected by Paul, not because he thinks humanity possesses none, but because he translates this immediately into independence from God. He freely attributes boastfulness both to Jewish observants and thorough worldlings. The chief perversion of gifts and capacities is to consider them as if one had them of oneself. Whatever capability humanity may have had for recognizing God through creatures, it has long since lost (cf. Rom 1:20f.; 1 Cor 1:21).

Paul ascribes reason and conscience to human beings without hesitation. They know as if by instinct what is required of them—namely, a life conformed to the will of God. They live instead lives of religiosity and conformity to ethical standards, sometimes immoral ones, doing their will because incapable on their own terms of doing God's. Yet if pagans live under consciousness of impending judgment, as Paul states (cf. Rom 2:15f.), so much the more must Jews.

Humanity is guided by "spirit" as its higher self—there is that much dualism in Paul. But humanity's spirit is as entangled in self-conflict as is its body. This leaves the term "flesh" as Paul's best designation for disobedient and recalcitrant humanity. At times it means simply creatureliness, occasionally desire, sexual as well as any other. Generally it is Paul's term for human nature that cannot or will not submit to the divine spirit. As a spiritual being and the crown of creation, the human creature expresses frustration and incompletion as if for the entire cosmos (cf. Rom 8:22). Even Christians have this experience, despite the pledge of the spirit in their hearts (cf. v. 23). Yet this divine spirit alone can help them in their weakness (cf. vv. 26f.).

Paul parallels "flesh" and "body" so frequently that the usage cannot be meaningless, even though all his anthropological terms describe the whole human creature. He asks for an offering of bodies in sacrifice for spiritual worship (cf. Rom 12:1), as he has done in a plea against lust (cf. 6:13f.). "For Paul, all God's ways with his creation begin and end with corporeality."[10] It is the linchpin of his soteriology, as the statement, "The body . . . is for the Lord, and the Lord is for the body" (1 Cor 6:13), underscores. The word "body" has eucharistic, ecclesiological, and christological reference at different times, indicating that Paul sees in humanity a creature that can be understood entirely in terms of body nature. Only in Rom 8:13 does he distinguish between the body and its "deeds," which are to be put to death "by the spirit." Even this is not the subject-object division it appears to be. It is an identity of spirit nature (subjection to God) versus carnal nature (resistance to God). The question is simply this: Is one to be under God's dominion or that of external forces?

Paul is committed to chaste conduct and is the sworn enemy of lust. This would be true of any rabbi of the time. We need not look to his chosen celibate career to explain it. He does not oppose marriage or favor universal abstention from sex. Careful exegesis of 1 Cor 7:1–16 discloses that he is tempering the excesses of some spiritualists who wish to forgo sex in marriage entirely, and encouraging others to proceed normally with their lives as they await the Lord's return. His major concern is voiced in v. 17: all should carry on as before, and not make hasty decisions in panic. In v. 7 ("I will all men to be as I am") he probably favors being undisturbed by troublesome passions and worry over what course of action to pursue. It is unthinkable that he wishes continence for all.

EXTERNAL EVIL FORCES

The "external forces" of the authentic Pauline letters are these: Satan (1 Thes 2:18; 2 Thes 2:9); the "god of this world" (2 Cor 4:4); the "secret force of lawlessness already at work" (2 Thes 2:7); and "every knee [which must bend at Jesus' name] in the heavens, on the earth, and under the earth" (Phil 2:10). Demonism has that much of a lively existence in Paul. It is developed further by his disciples into an influential host of "principalities and powers" (Col 1:16; 2:10). There is "the prince of the air, that spirit who is even now at work among the rebellious" (Eph 2:2). The same epistle speaks of "the rulers of this world of darkness, the evil spirits in regions above" (Eph 6:12). The demonic is real to Paul, but it is part of something larger, the rebellion of the highest creatures. He might even have termed it "flesh" if this were not so clearly a word for humanity.

These creatures are angelic in Hebrew categories. In Hellenistic, they are cosmic, reaching out to the stars and planets. In any case, the enslavement of humanity is their purpose. Insofar as they are successful, humanity experiences the self-contradiction of existence that cries out for redemption. The powers induce the human race to a rebellious existence. It may take the form of a perversion of "law, reason, history, existence and even the charismata."[11] They invite all humanity, even Christian believers, to an identity that is self-centered. Their influence on humanity is from without, their temptation is to a life lived within. For Paul, the true identity of human beings lies outside themselves. They are called by God to a life of spirit under the dominion of the risen Christ, who, with the destruction of the last enemy, death, will turn them over to him (1 Cor 15:20–28).

This picture is frankly mythical. So is the notion that Adam's sin is repeated and confirmed in every individual (cf. Rom 1:20ff.; 5:12ff.; 7:13ff.). This fact does not make Paul less than fully serious. Neither does it absolve the Christian from complete devotion to Paul's gospel once he has translated the myth for his own age. The vision is corporate as well as individual, therefore necessarily political and economic. It situates humanity's fulfillment outside itself, declaring that apart from God, Jesus as Lord, and the one Spirit of both, continued frustration lies in store.

"Flesh" is the real bodily existence of those who, tragically, look for salvation within themselves. It means something other in Paul than in the Bible, where it normally signifies the creature as contrasted with the Creator. Pauline "flesh" is all that is earthly circumstanced, labile, sure to be left behind. There will be a resurrection of the body, not of the flesh.

Again it is legitimate to ask how Paul came to look at things in this way, so uncharacteristic of Hebrew piety and thought. How could he write: "My point is that you should live in accord with the spirit and you will not yield to the cravings of the flesh. For the flesh lusts against the spirit and the spirit against the flesh; the two are directly opposed. This is why you do not do what your will intends" (Gal 5:16f.; cf. Rom 8: 1–11). Obviously he is not speaking of body and spirit in the Greek sense. His antithesis is between all that is of God and Christ and all that refuses this gentle dominion.

The Creator-creature distinction in Judaism was never an antithesis. Man was not set against God by definition, and certainly not God against man. Nor is that what Paul means by flesh versus spirit. It is creaturehood which will not serve versus the God who looks for obedient service. The mystery of demonic iniquity (cf. 2 Thes 2:7) and human sinfulness is explicable in terms of the polar opposite: the holiness of Christ become the justice of humanity.

This understanding of flesh, which was new even for a Hellenist Jew, caused Paul to read the remaining data in its light. The risen Christ was the epitome of obedient humanity, the "image of God" (2 Cor 4:4). We are predestined to share his image (cf. Rom 8:29). He was without sin, but by taking upon himself the full weight of the old eon he "became sin" (2 Cor 5:21). Paul saw a world in thrall to death and sin and implacably set against God as the reverse image of a humanity reconciled, the cosmic powers defeated, a potentially sinless "new creation." The reverse imagery was not biblical, but neither was the vision of a world redeemed through Jesus Christ.

Things might have gone quite differently for Paul. He could have outrun Johanan ben Zakkai and Judah ha Nasi in his devotion to the Law (cf. Phil 3:5f.) had he not experienced the risen Christ (cf. vv. 7–11). By his own account, this meeting with the Lord stood everything on its head. It was the alchemist's stone that turned riches to rubbish. "For his sake I have forfeited everything. . . . The justice I possess is that which comes through faith in Christ. It has its origin in God and is based on faith" (vv. 8–9).

Paul was not free of dualistic influences. But if he thought
in dualistic categories, they were his own. They were not the
spirit versus matter of the Greeks nor the light versus darkness of the Qumranites. They were a peculiarly Pauline spirit
versus flesh—all that is, in Christ, set against all that is not,
in its boastful self-centeredness and independence of God's
redemptive power.

The development is subtle and not fully consistent even in
Paul. It is no wonder that a Jewish world rejected it, and not
simply on grounds of Paul's hostility to the Judaism of his own
experience, which was not that of most Jews. Rather, it was
because his thoughts had no easily recognizable Jewish pedigree. Things might have gone better if his "flesh" were the
"flesh" of the Hebrew Scriptures, but it was not. Even Christians have coped poorly with the development of his
thought. The Gnostics read into his letters a straight metaphysical dualism which the church managed to reject.[12] But
the Greek-speaking church could not prevent flesh and spirit
from connoting what they would naturally connote to believers who knew no Jewish anthropology. Neither was the
church able to keep "law" and "sin" apart, nor did it wish to.
It lumped them together and laid them on the entire Jewish
people, which was far from Paul's intent.

The fact that Paul never praised nature, the cosmos, or the
human race does not mean that these had no worth for him.
They all had their provisional creaturely importance. They
had people to praise them in great numbers—diverting creatures from the Creator idolatrously, as Paul saw it. The principle, "Abuse does not take away use," was not a favorite with
him. He fulminated against the abuse of the world and of
man, which to him meant giving glory to anything other than
God in Christ. As to ignorance of this vital matter, whether
by the hypothetical good pagan or the actual good Jew, Paul
conducted himself like a jurist maintaining equivalently that
"ignorance is no excuse." His only policy was to bring all to
a knowledge of Christ.

Is Sin Inevitable?

It is one thing to consider Paul as one who does not think the cosmos evil except as led astray by angelic and human representatives who chose sin. To ask whether he thought sin was inevitable is another. It is still a third to inquire what he supposed God meant to do by giving the Law to Israel, and why the plan—however Paul conceived it—miscarried.

Whether or not sin was inevitable, there is no doubt that Paul regarded sin as a fact. He does not arrive at this notion speculatively, nor does he speculate upon it. He accounts for it as something primordial, identifying Adam as its ancestor. He could as easily have chosen the myth from Gn 6:4 to account for evil, but this might have led to the thought that the need for redemption did not precede the mysterious Nephilim. In fact, the need was universal because redemption in Christ was universal. That conviction was Paul's starting point. Speculation on whether Adam could have lived sinlessly, or how his sin became our sin, is absent both from Genesis and from Paul. The apostle simply states what to him are incontrovertible propositions: humanity is sinful and always has been; and it is fitting to identify our father in sin once we have identified Christ, through whom we are begotten in grace.

If we must speculate, the moral impossibility of a human life free of sin seems to be the soundest speculation. Moral impossibility is not necessity. There is no indication in the Hebrew or Christian Scriptures that human beings must sin, if sin means to choose consciously and radically against God. The Bible amply attests that people are free and yet do sin. "If you do well, you can hold up your head; but if not, sin is a demon lurking at the door: his urge is toward you, yet you can be his master" (Gn 4:7). In Eden, Adam and his wife are not set apart from other human beings as incapable of sin. The opposite is true. The naming of birds and beasts (cf.

2:20), their lack of shame though they were naked (cf. v. 25), their new awareness of shame after disobedience (cf. 3:7), and the sentence to hardship that followed disobedience (cf. vv. 16–19, 23f.) are intended to explain many things—death, sexuality, and drudgery. They do not explain the origins of a relative moral incapacity. The possibility of sin was present from the beginning.

Even the exclamation of the LORD about the Man's becoming "like one of us, knowing what is good and what is bad" (Gn 3:22), does not describe the dawn of moral discernment in humanity or the tragic effects of sin, as is so often said. The reason why the Man must not have access to the second tree is that it could provide him with immortality (v. 22). His "knowing good and bad" has to do with being fully in possession of mental and physical powers, an awareness of the generative process in particular.[13] It was in this that he "has become like one of us." The accusation that man has put himself in God's place will occur again in a context of power, not sex, against the kings of Tyre (Ezek 28:2, 6) and, less specifically, against the kings of Babylon (Is 14:10–15).

We must conclude, therefore, that whereas this tale means to account for the origins of death, human misery, the need for clothing, and sexual awareness, it does not set itself to explain the possibility of disobeying God. That was there from the beginning. The only thing that was not present was its logical consequences. Sin always brings disastrous consequences. The difference in this case is that death is one of them.

The rabbis and Philo stressed the tragic results of Adam's sin, not the sin itself.[14] Humanity not only became mortal but subject to fear and pain. Beauty of appearance was lost, physical and mental abilities were impaired. Paul confines himself to a single human result of sin—namely, death—but he does not hesitate to mention certain cosmic outcomes as well: "Creation was made subject to futility [connoting evil spiritual beings], not of its own accord but by him who once subjected it [Adam? Satan? perhaps God].... [Yet] the world itself will be freed from its slavery to corruption" (Rom 8: 20f.). This connotation reflects the prevailing rabbinic outlook, which was convinced that the world was populated with principalities and powers that were set against God and whose disobedience was somehow connected with the sin of man.[15] The rabbis focused less on the person of Adam than on all that followed in the train of his sin. Neither did he have any glorious personal future. At the end-time, all that Adam lost would be restored, not to him but to the entire race.

Did Paul think that ever since the first sin the human race was under the necessity of sinning? Two statements of his highlight this question: "We know that the law is spiritual, whereas I am weak flesh sold into the slavery of sin" (Rom 7: 14), and, "My inner self agrees with the law of God, but I see in my body's members another law at war with the law of my mind; this makes me the prisoner of the law of sin in my members" (vv. 22f.). Allowing for the force of rhetoric in what are patently not meant to be dogmatic statements, the apostle wishes to describe by a "law of sin in my members" a state of internal conflict common to all. It is pressing his meaning too far to say that each member of the race is under necessity to sin, or that there has been no freedom since Adam in any real sense of that word.

Paul is describing human life as a battleground in which there are as many losses as victories. Gentiles and Jews alike are under God's judgment because they are "under sin" (Rom 3:9). Only God's grace in Christ saves (vv. 22, 24–26), since it provides a way out of the fact of sin and its consequences. That "all have sinned and are deprived of the glory of God" (v. 23) is the factual situation since Adam. The redemption wrought in Christ Jesus (v. 24) is no less as fact. But there is no reason to say that Paul holds that all humanity sins necessarily. If all chose to sin freely, his terms "law of sin," "slavery of sin," and "under sin" would still stand. A person who consistently opts for an evil course of action may exist in a captive state.

SIN AS COSMIC ALIENATION

This brings us to a central point in Pauline theology: Is sin an act of disobedience against God's law of love or is it the sum total of such acts? It seems to be neither. For that Paul uses terms such as "the breaking of a precept" (Rom 5:14; Gal 5:19) or "transgression" (Rom 5:15, 17f., 20). "Sin," both because it is regularly personified and dealt with as an implacable reality by Paul, does not so much designate individual moral fault as describe the total wrenching away of the cosmos from its Creator. Sin is the condition of the world as it ought not to be, as opposed to the world as it ought to be, a state summed up by "grace." The difference for Paul resides in "faith": again, not so much an individual state of heart but an enabling device of God's doing to open the entire cosmos to the lordship of Christ.

Paul is interested in real individuals, but his concern for them is as something of Adam or Christ, of sin or grace, of wrath or reconciliation. The two ages are the matters of great consequence—God's just response to sinners which is judgment and his merciful initiative toward their sin which is reconciliation. That persons commit real sins, there can be no doubt. But their alienated state occupies Paul far more than the pitiful infractions that come of it. He is not terribly interested in individual acts of wrongdoing. He is interested in the cosmic rebellion that surfaces only in those creatures, angelic and human, who mean to put themselves in God's place. He is interested, above all, in the obedient man Jesus Christ, who places himself before God as man should do: docile, open, ready to serve.

We can now examine why Paul thought that Mosaic Law was powerless to set Israel right with God, when the chief legitimate tradition of the times was that it did that very thing. The human plight, as Paul sees it, is so profound that it goes to the roots of human and cosmic being. It is not something that can be mended by God's act of forgiveness after human repentance—the ordinary way of rectification in Jewish thought. Paul is not interested in how the Galatians may be forgiven by God after their transgressions but in how they may avoid falling back into *bondage* (Gal 4:8; 5:1), once given their freedom in Christ (5:1) and the Spirit (3:1–5). This freedom of theirs which is a righteousness is a totally new condition in Christ succeeding a former one.[16]

In the Tannaitic period, the rabbis were convinced that the matter of salvation for Jews had been settled by God's decree of merciful election. What is clearest of all is that he chose Israel "for his own sake."[17] As a consequence of their election God gave the Israelites commandments that required obedience. This obedience was the proper response to him within the terms of the covenant. It was not the means of salvation. There were no such means apart from God's free choice, which culminated in the giving of the covenant. As king, he gave his people the benefits of deliverance from Egypt, sustenance in the desert, and victory in the battle with Amalek. Having redeemed them from Egypt, he then gave commandments, which they undertook to obey.

There is great stress on reward and punishment in the writings of the rabbis. Obedience brings the first, disobedience the second. Yet there is never a precise correspondence spelled out between salvation and success in keeping the Law. God remains faithful; he does not go back on his covenant even when the Jews transgress the Law. His fidelity is independent of their response. It is possible to throw off the yoke of the Law, but while one remains within a covenantal framework some means of atonement for sin can be found. Temple sacrifices were one such means. The rites of Yom Kippur were another. After the temple was destroyed, various second-century A.D. systems were devised to ensure forgiveness. Inconsistent with one another as they were, they did not impair the general principle: there is a way to atone for every transgression committed after the initial election.

Since the Jews of the Tannaitic period were convinced that

they were saved, they did not "pursue" salvation. They had various opinions on how gentiles were to be saved, some holding for charity and others for the Noachian precepts. Still others, like Rabbi Joshua, thought that since there were no righteous among the gentiles, none could be saved.

While Paul retains the whole rabbinic scheme on sins and repentance for them, he never mentions forgiveness. Instead, at points where we might expect it, he says that we are "made righteous by faith" (Rom 5:1) or are "in Christ" (8:1). We are "in the flesh" (7:5f.), "slaves of sin" (6:20), "under the law" (Gal 4:4), in a condition of "slavery which leads to death" (Rom 6:16). The opposite to all this is freedom, salvation, and life. To be made righteous is, for Paul, to be constituted a new creation, not obeying the Law and atoning for transgression.[18] Righteousness is not a maintained or even a restored state, but a fundamental change from death to life. For Paul, election constitutes a renewal of the Abrahamic covenant but not for a people *en bloc,* only for those who ratify it in faith. Everyone was under condemnation, in Paul's view, until the coming of the new situation which offered salvation to all.

In Paul's epistle to the Romans his ideas on justification are brought to a peak. This letter is usually divided in this way: Rom 1–8 deal with the sinful condition of humanity and God's action to deliver it in Christ; 9–11 consider the place of Israel in the total salvation scheme; and 12–15 point up the implications of humanity's graced condition in Paul's churches, which he communicates to the church at Rome. His discussion of the bondage in which the human race finds itself is factual and experiential, much like the enslavement of the Jews in Egypt. The book of Exodus provided no rationale for what took place. It described the grim facts of Jewish life, then told how deliverance came. Similarly, Paul documents gentile slavery to sin, as any pagan moralist might do, coupling it with Jewish defections from the Law (1:18–3:20). He is not insensitive to the power of conscience in the gentile (2:14ff.) or of the Law in the life of the Jew (2:29). He expects that those who keep the Law, whether by way of conscience or letter, will be declared just in the sight of God (2:13). Yet Jew and gentile alike are under God's judgment.

THE LAW REVEALS SIN

God is no less merciful or forgiving now than before, but the magnitude of human sinfulness has come home to Paul in a way that is uncharacteristic of the Judaism of the time. He compiles a catalog of human perfidy from the Psalms, Proverbs, and Third Isaiah (Rom 3:10b–18; cf. Pss 14:1ff.; 5: 10; 140:4; 10:7; Is 59:7; Prv 1:16; Ps 36:2). Instead of proclaiming the terms of repentance and forgiveness, he states that "no one will be justified in God's sight through observance of the Law; the Law does nothing but point out what is sinful" (Rom 3:20).

It is not unusual for moralists to declare that theirs are the worst of times. If that were all Paul was doing, we could understand it. But he has arrived at the novel conclusion that Law observance (including observance by way of conscience) yields Law justification only, which is not enough. It is not justification in the full sense. Human falsehood only brings to light God's truth (Rom 3:7). Human wrongdoing provides proof of God's justice (v. 5). This justice had heretofore been manifested through the Law, and Jews were right in thinking that there was to be no fuller embodying of it until the last age. Presumably Paul had not always held Abrahamic faith to be superior to Mosaic observance. The difference has been made by "that justice of God which works through faith in Jesus Christ for all who believe" (v. 22). In other words, the availability of God's justice in relative fullness as a human possession has come to light lately, forcing Paul to think hard about two things: the superabundant generosity of the solution to the human plight and the enormity of the plight that required such a solution.

If Paul had not been faced throughout his career of preach-

ing with fellow Jews who would not accept his gospel, he
might have worked out a theory of peaceful transition from
law to gospel. His statement that he was confirming the Law,
not abolishing it (Rom 3:31), Matthean in its ring, might have
prevailed in Christian memory over the one that stands out:
"For we hold that a man is justified by faith apart from observance of the Law" (v. 28). It is impossible to say what
tipped the balance. The evidence from his letters suggests
two things: He came to identify all claims for Law observance, as opposed to the need to believe in Christ, as "boast-
ing," and to characterize all observance as conformity to a
"Law of works" (v. 27). What at first had not been an antithesis in Paul's mind but a transition in virtue of God's new deed
probably became an antithesis because his opponents made
it so. Or so it seems he would have claimed. He made strenuous efforts to establish that God cannot contradict himself.
The Law, he says, had been God's means to identify sin.
Surely this was a new conception calculated to minimize the
Law. But Paul would say it was accurate. Human sinfulness,
a personified reality, had then taken over and perverted the
Law.

If the justice of God was manifested to enslaved Israel in
Egypt apart from the Law, so too had it been in Abraham's
time (Rom 4:3; cf. Gn 15:6). Just what Paul means by the
"justice of God" in Rom 3:21 is not clear. There is some
ground for thinking that it has a covenant rather than a legal
significance.[19] In Genesis, Abraham responds to God's call
and promise as the people Israel will do in Exodus. Accepting
God's offer was an indication of loyalty and trust. Its result is
his covenant righteousness given as a gracious gift. God's
election love comes first. Abraham's justice credited to him
(Rom 4:3) represents the patriarch's acceptance of God's
choice and his decision to go wherever that choice would
take him.

Paul sees redemption in Christ similarly. It is an expression
of God's love through Christ's sacrifice which is equally an
acceptance of God's choice. Only through acceptance of this

sacrifice by God could the sin of the world be taken away. Paul writes that the biblical words about Abraham's faith credited to him as righteousness (Rom 4:23; cf. Gn 15:6) were intended for later generations. "For our faith will be credited to us also if we believe in him who raised Jesus our Lord from the dead, the Jesus who was handed over to death for our sins and raised up for our justification" (vv. 24f.).

Paul is under no illusion that there will be no more sin in human life. It is just that in the present epoch, for those who "believe in him," the power of sin is rendered ineffectual. Even death has been overcome, ultimately. God has effected what human effort could never have achieved. But it is not as if humanity had no part in it. Not all are delivered, only those who believe, in an acceptance like Abraham's of the same justifying covenant love. The result is "peace with God through our Lord Jesus Christ" (Rom 5:1), in place of our former condition of powerlessness (v. 6), subjection to God's wrath (v. 9) and his enmity (v. 10).

The balance that was lost through sin and its punishment of death (cf. Rom 5:12–14) has been restored through "the grace of God and the gracious gift of one man, Jesus Christ" (v. 15). One act of disobedience made sinners of all: the Adam epoch. One superabounding act of obedience will constitute "the many" just: the Christ epoch (v. 19). Paul cannot forbear pointing a reproachful finger at the Law, which in his view could not leave bad enough alone. It made sin to be "sins" and in that sense "increased" it (v. 20).

Paul wants to underscore the marvelous imbalance between Christ's one deed and humanity's many sinful deeds. Otherwise the wonder of the divine mercy might go unrecognized. Christ's victory over the fierce power of sin was for all time to come. The transgressions of Jews under the Law were but a tiny part of the staggering total. Yet, as Paul saw it, they were impressive when set against a background of misplaced faith in the Law's power to save. He therefore chose to describe the Law in negative rather than neutral or positive terms.

The restored cosmic balance continues to be stressed in Rom 6, with the image of sin-death versus justification-life. Christ lives; unrepeatable death is behind him (6:9). The progress he made (v. 10) in his death to sin (therefore to flesh, to the old eon) was unto "life for God" (the condition of all who would have it so in the new eon). This progress of Christ must be matched by a similar death-life transition in the baptized (vv. 3–8, 11). Paul knows well the misunderstandings this kind of teaching has caused in Corinth, with its attendant antinomianism. He acknowledges the risk (vv. 1–2). Yet he can think of no better way to describe the reality that underlies the symbol of burial in baptismal waters than to call it a passage from death to life (vv. 3–4). Turning to the figure of slavery, he counsels the Romans to become "slaves of God" (v. 22) now that being "slaves of sin" is over (v. 20).

SIN PERSISTS IN THE NEW EPOCH

Nothing should be allowed to mitigate the grandeur of Paul's conception. In fact, however, the failure to read it for the myth it is in praise of God's initiating love has led to antinomian interpretations like the very ones he deplores: the saved who cannot be lost; those who cannot sin because they are no longer "in sin." Almost immediately after Paul's day, the church resumed the Pharisaic practice of giving attention to individual transgressions and the means to achieve forgiveness of them. Rather than a regrettable "re-Judaizing of Christianity," this development represents a realistic awareness that the justified are capable of lapse and that God will forgive the transgressions of sinners. Paul faced this possibility in his various exhortations to his converts to stand fast in the faith. (Cf. Gal 3:3, where he grants that anyone who has "begun in the spirit" can revert to "the flesh.") He is elated that the epoch of sin and death is succeeded by that of grace and life. He concentrates far more on the divine power which has achieved this than on the human weakness which refuses to come wholeheartedly into the new age.

Christian generations have failed to heed Paul's teaching in two ways: by presuming on God's grace or despairing of his power. As to the second, they have not sufficiently acknowledged what he has done in them and foolishly relied on themselves. Regarding the first, they have so concentrated on what he has done that they have neglected to acknowledge what they must do. Pauline "faith" is not a meritorious "work," but it is both divine gift and human activity. Just as sins are possible to the justified in the new age by dint of their freedom, so faith will be a reality to them only if, like Abraham, they respond in freedom. God's grace cannot be praised by disregarding human freedom. Christians, misreading Paul's letters, have been doing this for centuries. They have assumed that his praise of God's abounding grace has meant an alteration of human nature. They were now capable of a kind of response that humanity was incapable of before. Or they were now invulnerable to sin. Paul teaches none of these things. He pleads for a free response to the one covenant love that has lately been expressed in cross and resurrection.

The key to the puzzling seventh chapter of Romans lies in v. 6. "Newness of spirit" is the Christ epoch and the "antiquity of letter" the Adam epoch, typified by the text of Mosaic Law. Once this succession of ages is understood, Paul becomes clearer. Once again the function of the Law is to apprise the Jews of the human situation which is one of sin. The Law simply informs about it and specifies what the transgressions are. In a kind of Lange-James theory ("The man was not frightened because he saw the bear, he saw the bear because he was frightened"), Paul has the Law identifying and activating sin rather than responding to it. His "I" which came to know sin, then to be deceived and killed by the knowledge (7:7–11), is the "I" in whose members two laws engage in mortal struggle. It represents not the autobiographical Paul, but human beings everywhere. The new eon has succeeded the old, yet the internal conflict has not passed. The "law of sin" (v. 23) continues to hold all mankind under the "power of death" (v. 24) until "flesh" yields to "mind," which in this case is spirit, the spirit of God, the spirit of Christ in the new age. The battle is over to the degree that faith is admitted. It continues to the degree that it is resisted.

There are not two Laws of God, Mosaic and Christian. There is a law of sin which the one Law of God overcomes. It is a law of submission to the power of divine spirit, not claims of victory located in a law of human flesh. The Law of Moses as appriser of sin becomes the Law of spirit (Rom 8: 2) as vanquisher of sin.

Chapter 8 continues the argument. Any power the Mosaic Law might have had is negated by disobedient "flesh" (8:3, 7). The work of God, on which Paul has been concentrating, now gives place to a discussion of how this saving work is to be appropriated. The answer: by living according to the spirit (v. 4). That means the just demand of God, which for Paul is faith in Christ. The spirit of him who raised Christ from the dead dwells in those who belong to Christ (v. 9). This indwelling spirit will bring the mortal bodies of believers to life (v. 11), both in a future resurrection and in a present termination of fleshliness, the "deeds of the body" (v. 13). Adoption, sonship, and inheritance of God are in prospect (vv. 14–16). Glory is to be achieved through suffering (vv. 17–18). The whole creation is in travail. It groans because slavery to corruption is still the reality of this age (vv. 20–23). Yet hope is sure, even though its object is not seen (vv. 24–25). No condemnation is in store for the predestined, least of all at the hands of God or Christ, from whom they successively receive a calling, justification, glory (vv. 28–34). The outcome is certain. For those who continue to exercise the human acts of faith, hope, and endurance, neither earthly trials nor superhuman "powers" can "separate us from the love of God that comes to us in Christ Jesus, our Lord" (v. 39).

The past fifty years have been crowded with efforts to demythologize the gospels if they are to be believed. A soberer view sees the need to accept their mythical element whether on its terms or ours. The powerful myth of the two Pauline epochs—that of letter and spirit, law and grace, sin and righteousness, death and life—requires the same treatment if Christian faith is to live its own life and not a parasitic existence of anti-Jewishness.

WHAT PAUL MEANS BY LAW AND GRACE

For too long the antithetical ages have been historicized, as if Paul were primarily interested in an epoch of Judaism succeeded by an epoch of Christianity. He is not, as a careful exegesis of Rom 9–11 will disclose. He is concerned with two diametrically opposed spirits, trust in God or trust in self, reliance on his deed or reliance on our deeds. He has found the latter spirit exemplified by those who boast in works of the Law—but they are not all who are Jews nor are they only Jews. He knows that those who have faith in Christ are not all who make up the churches, nor are they all non-Jews. In developing his theory, he has let his examples get in the way of his principles. The teaching church cannot allow the confusion to continue with its grandiose—and often quite wrong—contrasts between the law and the gospel.

The correct contrast is between the law of sin and the law of grace. Either can flourish under Mosaic Law or gospel. Paul must be rephrased by a church that has his letters to say clearly what he says obscurely. The deed of Christ may no longer be praised at the price of deprecating the Mosaic deliverance. The Law and its commandments identify the power of sin but they do more than that. If adhered to in fidelity, they are the Law of the spirit of God. They are the Law of Christ in embryo, because the spirit that enlivens both is the same spirit, the spirit of the one God who does not change.

The three chapters of Romans concerned with the Jewish people (Rom 9–11) contain the same familiar themes we have

found in the earlier part of the epistle. These are God's free
choice of a people for reasons that seem good to him (9:15;
cf. Ex 33:19), his deliverance of that people from slavery so
that the whole earth may ring with praise of his power (9:17;
cf. Ex 9:16), and the separation of a remnant from the midst
of a whole people (9:27, 29; 11:5; cf. Is 10:22; 1:9) or the
creation of a people from those who had not been a people
(9:25–26; cf. Hos 2:25).

Throughout these chapters there is found the notion of
God's mercy (9:23) or kindness (11:22), but also of his utter
gratuity (11:5–6). All precede any particular decisions he has
made. They have resulted in deliverance from the Pharaoh,
the creation of Israel as "my people," the salvation of a remnant, the giving of a Law (9:4; 10:5), and now the constitution
of a people of faith (9:32; 10:6, 10, 17) made up of Jews and
gentiles (9:24; 10:12). Subsequent generations of Christians,
like Augustine and John Calvin, saw in this ninth chapter
with its biblical examples a double predestination of the
human race to glorification and condemnation.[20] A careful
study discloses, however, the predestination of all to mercy
and reconciliation, with the disobedience of some for a certain season, to achieve the ultimate divine purpose.

Paul does not consider God's latest action in history inconsistent or unexpected. The LORD has proceeded in a straight
line and announced at all points what he meant to do. He
does not and cannot repent of his choice of the Israelites (9:
13). His "gifts and his call are irrevocable" (11:29). Theirs are
the promises and the patriarchs (9:4f.). Forever they are the
root, the trunk, and the natural branches of the olive tree (11:
15–21). The present offense of some of them is unbelief (10:
14, 21; 11:20) and disobedience (11:31) as it was of old (10:21).
God has not broken his covenant. As deliverer he will come
from Zion "and remove from Jacob all impiety" (11:26f.; cf.
Is 59:20f.).

The Jews have temporarily become the enemies of God in
respect to the gospel—while remaining beloved of him because of the patriarchs (11:28). He has held out his justice to

them and they have sought to establish their own justice (10: 3). "Have they not heard [the gospel]?" Paul asks. He answers that they have (10:18). But, as in Isaiah's day, not all have believed it (10:16; cf. 53:1). God has chosen a people by grace, not by works (11:6). The response to this choice directed to Jew and Greek alike (10:12) is in the realm of faith. "Justice comes from faith, not from works." This explains why Israel, "seeking a law from which justice would come, did not arrive at that law" (9:31, 32). Whoever responds to God's call in faith (for Paul, faith in Christ)—Jew or Greek, it makes no difference—receives the justice that means salvation (10:10).

The argument is not without its obscurities. One is forced to say on balance that in making it Paul was unintentionally self-defeating. Had he been content with God's overall design whereby gentile faith necessarily derives from Jewish, or maintained that the Law was meant to flower in yet further covenantal gratuity, he would have been on safe ground. But Jewish resistance to the gospel was a fact of his experience. He felt it had to be explained. He did so in terms of other Israelite resistance from the past, capping it with an ingenious theory of Jewish envy at gentile riches (11:11–12)—a situation which never came to pass on any large scale in Jewish life.

In these three chapters of Romans, descriptive of the epoch of grace in Christ which succeeds God's graciousness to Abraham and the people of the exodus, the Law is not set against faith. Faith yields *its* justice; a certain type of response to the Law yields *its* justice. The Law as responded to in Abrahamic faith never comes up for discussion. This is, in a sense, Hamlet played without the prince of Denmark. Was it that Paul never experienced such a reality, or encountered it so little—and its opposite so much—that it had no existence for him? Perhaps. Or could it be that the logic of its outworking would have destroyed his careful balance? His Roman readers were a community made up of Jews and gentiles alike who had justifying faith. However, he argues his case for this faith in such a way that they were forever submerged by the partial and inaccurate picture he gives of a gentile people that had it, and an Israel (11:7) or Jews (vv. 23, 28) that did not.

The next three chapters (12:1–15:13) are of great importance on the way in which a local church lives out in practice that righteousness which results from God's justification. Paul knows that a whole set of choices—we call it a life-style —is incumbent on a people of faith. The concluding part of Romans is as complete a program, in its way, as is the sermon on the mount. Far more than the lists of virtues and vices or moral exhortations that appear elsewhere in Paul's letters, this treatment answers the question: How are faith and ethics, the indicative and the imperative, related in Paul? His answer lies in the realm of faith's proper response to the divine favor that has taken the initiative. Self-offering in sacrifice, in a spiritual worship, is indicated (cf. 12:1). This will take the form of a modest estimate of one's importance, mutual support in virtue of individual gifts, sincere love, conformity to the legitimate demands of the state, concern for the weak, and tolerance of those who differ. "Everything written before our time was written for our instruction, that we might derive hope from the lessons of patience and the words of encouragement in the Scriptures" (15:4). There, a non-polemical Paul speaks who knows that none of God's words in the Law can be lost. His prayer is that God will enable believers to live in perfect harmony (v. 5). The justified may expect continual divine aid in living lives of righteousness that derive from faith. They must keep all the commandments, which are summed up in love of one's neighbor (13:8–10).

SUMMARY

The indisputable facts for the life of the church that emerge from Paul's epistles, especially from Romans, are the following:

—He is a Hellenized and an apocalyptic Jew but thoroughly a Jew, hence not to be dismissed as "spiritual" in the Greek manner or disinterested in the affairs of this life because he expected Christ's return in glory. To view Jewish eon thought as disinterested in the present life is to historicize myth, thereby failing to comprehend it.

—The basic mythic structure underlying Pauline thought is the Jewish one of "this age" and "the age to come," with the onset of the latter anticipated by the resurrection of Christ. Any antitheses Paul sets up, e.g., as between letter and spirit, sin and death and justification and life, or law and grace are elaborations which have meaning in terms of the myth rather than any ethical reality in the lives of individual Jews and non-Jews or those peoples corporately.

—A correspondence of the terms of Pauline myth with ethical reality is possible if individuals in community appropriate Christ's life to their own, but its primary significance is the cosmic deed of God over the ages in angelic and human existence.

—Whereas finding the origins of human mortality in the sin of Adam was natural to Paul, the notion may not come readily to other ages any more than will the image of solidarity in sin with the "first sinner." The specifics of the biblical tale are not only not essential to Pauline eon thought but may interfere with it; to know that humanity in its freedom has chosen against God from the beginning is to believe in original sin in the only way the Hebrew Bible or Paul teaches it.

—"The Law" in Paul most often refers to the observance of specified precepts as saving, put forward polemically in opposition to acceptance of Jesus as the Messiah. Even when the Law is viewed in itself, such overtones are never entirely absent. Hence, God's grace in Jesus Christ opposes diametrically the mentality in pagan, Jew, or Christian of the Law thus understood, whereas it completes the covenant gift of Sinai; the God of Moses cannot be thought of as having yielded to the Father of Jesus Christ who acts differently from him.

—The essential Jewishness of Paul must be retained if the church is to understand him.

—The church may not conceive of itself in any way but as Paul did—namely, a community of believers in which gentiles are mercifully admitted to the company of Jews who are sons and daughters of the promise.

—There is no such thing as a church made up of gentiles in improved or superior condition to the Jews who remain faithful to the covenant and the Law.

—There is no such thing as a church which is all grace and a Jewish people which is all Law. Both are realities of grace and law, fulfilling their destinies in the measure in which they perceive them and are faithful to them.

—God knows how to bring good out of evil and faith out of unbelief, so that the state of mind of Paul's Jewish contemporaries is to be viewed as contributing to a higher divine purpose to be revealed in his good time.

Chapter IV

BEYOND THE SYNOPTICS
AND PAUL

The Johannine gospel and epistles are widely thought to epitomize the demands of grace and love that come with the new dispensation. The epistles of James, Jude, and 2 Peter, conversely, have puzzled many generations by their "backsliding," as it were, into Jewish ways, while 1 Peter contains teaching that is largely Pauline. This chapter will set itself to sorting out the measure in which these writings are favorable or unfavorable to the Law. It will also attempt to see what happens to the world in the Christian outlook, as a result of Johannine strictures on "the world."

James, the "brother of Jesus who was called the Christ," is reported by Josephus as martyred in A.D. 62.[1] The letter that bears his name (Jas 1:1) had a hard time being accepted into the canon and was accepted only after apostolic identification was acknowledged.[2] The canonical "epistle" is scarcely in that genre. It is a collection of hortatory aphorisms in letter form composed in quite good Greek and depending on the Septuagint Bible. Its tone so much resembles that of Jewish wisdom literature that toward the end of the last century Friedrich Spitta was hypothesizing that the name of Christ had simply been inserted into a Jewish writing in two places (Jas 1:1; 2:1). A. Meyer in his *Riddle of James* worked out an elaborate theory in which a Christian hand recast a Jewish writing that had been patterned after the Testament of the Twelve Patriarchs, the sons of Jacob or James.[3]

The writing is more probably a Christian Jewish original

composed somewhere in Palestine or Syria by a person committed to a "piety of the poor" (cf. Jas 1:9; 2:1-7; 5:1-6). It is
not so extreme as to be identified with the Ebionites ("the
poor"), those Jewish believers in Jesus who reportedly separated themselves from gentile Christians. Its teaching is in
the spirit of Jesus' sayings on poverty or Luke's linking of
Jesus' birth and ministry with the lowly and despised elements of Jewish society.[4]

JAMES'S ETHICAL EXHORTATION

James is a chain of sayings and brief treatments in an ethical vein. The sole exception is a polemic against claims in
behalf of a "faith" that is professed but not practiced (Jas 2:
14-26). This brief sortie into the way salvation is accomplished cannot be compared with Paul's extensive theoriz-
ing. On superficial examination it seems to be in direct contradiction to what Paul affirms.

There are a number of likenesses in James to sayings of
Jesus. For example, we find beatitudes (Jas 1:12; 5:11), asking
for good gifts (1:5, 17; cf. Mt 7:7ff.), the contrast between
hearers and doers of the word (1:22; cf. Mt 7:24ff.), warnings
to avoid passing judgment (4:12; cf. Mt 7:1) and taking oaths
(5:12; cf. Mt 5:37), prayer without doubting (1:6; cf. Mk 11:
23f.), and laughter that will be turned into mourning (4:9; cf.
Lk 6:25). None of these is close enough to the Matthean or
Marcan formulation of a saying of Jesus to warrant a theory
of dependence on the gospels, but jointly they suggest access
to a common stock of sayings.

As to the supposedly non-Christian character of the epistle,
there are a number of features in it that make sense only if
it is Christian in origin. It also contains certain phrasing that
is uncharacteristic of the Jewish speech of the period that has
come down to us. With regard to the first matter, there is a
distinctively baptismal homily ring to, "He wills to bring us
to birth with a word spoken in truth so that we may be a kind

of firstfruits of his creatures" (Jas 1:18) and "the implanted word, with its power to save you" (v. 21). "The perfect law of freedom" sounds as if it may have a Christian history, as do the phrases, "the honored name that has been invoked upon you" (2:7) and the statement, "the coming of the Lord draws near" (5:8). Yet they are equally open to a Jewish interpretation. Prayer and the anointing of the sick by elders is conceivably a Jewish practice but not the phrase "the elders of the church" of 5:14. Much of the remaining hortatory material has parallels in Jewish and Greek sources indiscriminately.

The epistle contains no compelling reason to be considered late except the death date of James of Jerusalem. Some, like W. Michaelis, G. Kittel, and recently J. A. T. Robinson, reckon it the earliest of the extant Christian writings. Many have taken its passage on faith to be a response to the Pauline concept of justification that is being badly lived out. But there have been others, like Donald Guthrie, who think that Paul was responding to a misunderstood James.[5] Actually, there is insufficient evidence from this letter to say that it was written in direct refutation of Paul or that it is so clearly pre-Pauline that Paul could have been taking issue with it.

The theological problem between the two writers first surfaced in 1522 with Luther's claim that this was an "epistle of straw [which] has in it no quality of the gospel." The Reformer thought that it preached not Christ but the Law, that it taught justification by works, and that it was disorganized and "Jewish" even though right faith in God and some sound moral teaching were to be found in it. It is doubtful that Luther would have argued so vigorously against James if it did not seem to advocate in ch. 2 the necessity of works as supplementary to faith (2:21) or even faith in subordination to them ("faith was both assisting [Abraham's] works and was implementing his works," v. 22). In the main, James is made up of paraenetic elements with which Paul's epistles abound and which comprise the main thrust of Jesus' ethical sayings in the synoptics.

DEEDS AND FAITH BELONG TOGETHER

The author of James asks his readers, who are people of faith (Jas 1:3), to petition God for wisdom in faith, never doubting (vv. 5f.). He admonishes them in a variety of seemingly unconnected ways. They should rejoice in the testing of their faith in patient endurance, knowing that God tempts no one but gives good gifts that culminate in the crown of life to those who love him (vv. 2–18). The word of God should be listened to, but, above all, acted upon (vv. 19–27). To favor the rich over the poor is reprehensible; the corrective lies in loving one's neighbor as oneself; this sums up the "kingly law" (2:1, 11). The best preparation for judgment under the law of liberty is the exercise of mercy which triumphs over judgment (vv. 12f.). Abraham and Rahab gave proof of their faith and were justified by their works (cf. vv. 21, 23, 25). Such is the writer's biblical evidence against a faith that is lifeless because it does nothing in practice (vv. 14–26).

The tongue should be guarded, above all by those who teach (Jas 3:1–12). Heavenly wisdom is to be sought, not earthly cunning (vv. 13–18). Inner cravings and jealousies cannot lead to peace; those who walk humbly will be raised high (4:1–10). The slanderer contravenes the Law and is no observer of it, setting himself against the one Lawgiver and Judge who can save and destroy (vv. 11f.). The merchant or other person who plans his future without respect to God's will is presumptuous (vv. 13–16). Bad faith defines all sin (v. 17). The rich are to be presumed guilty of oppressing the poor; a bitter fate awaits them (5:1–6). Patience like that of Job should mark those who look for the coming of the Lord (vv. 7–11). Swearing any oath at all can bring condemnation (v. 12). The prayer of faith like that of Elijah can be efficacious, both in healing the sick and in mutual confession of sins (vv. 13–18). Efforts to bring back the erring brother can "cover a multitude of sins" (vv. 19f.; cf. Prv 10:12).

The counsel that James gives may be disjointed, but its content is not unlike that of Jesus in Mt 5–7 or Paul in Rom 12–15, especially 12:9–21. Indeed, if it were not distinguished from the Pauline writings by its advocacy of works on a par with faith, it would simply be noted as the NT's sole collection of exclusively paraenetic materials. What brings it to special notice is Jas 2:24: "You must perceive that a person is justified by his works and not by faith alone." This seems to go counter to Rom 3:28, even though Paul never uses the adverb "alone." There he writes: "For we hold that a man is justified by faith apart from observance of the Law."

Rather than turning immediately to that theological question as if it comprised the epistle's sole interest, it should be pointed out that a prior interest attaches to its more general characteristics. The author is a Christian and a moralist. He employs the epigrammatic style of the Jewish wisdom literature in the Hebrew and Greek canons of Scripture. He does not think ethical postures inconsequential, despite his assumption that the coming of the Lord is "at hand" (Jas 5:8). The latter eschatological expression is common in the synoptics. On the contrary, ethical questions are his great concern. His interests are Jewish in the manner of Jesus and Paul, which means that he, like them, is Hellenized. For James, God has certain expectations of people which they are able to fulfill: humility, trust, resistance to the passions, decency in speech. They can and must avoid envy, favoritism to the rich, and quarrels. At all points human freedom is assumed, enlightened by a wisdom from above for which one must ask (1:5; 3:17). Obedience to God and closeness to him are supreme values (4:7f.) He has given a Law and expects it to be kept (4:11f.). Sin, understood as the transgression of the Law's commands, is possible and must be avoided. The Law convicts its transgressors (2:9). It has about it an indivisible quality which renders a person guilty on all counts (2:10) who has sinned against one of its points. Paul holds this (Gal 3:10, citing Dt 27:26), and it was the teaching of some of the rabbis.

"You shall love your neighbor as yourself" (Jas 2:8; cf. Lv

19:18) epitomizes the Law, even as the care of orphans and widows and the avoidance of worldly stain constitutes true religion or devotion (1:26f.). The person who wrote James has in common with other NT authors and Jesus himself a radical interpretation of the Law, scaling it down from many precepts to a paradigmatic few. Yet the "ten words" still hold (2:11). The biblical assumptions about morality are fully in control. Human beings are free. God is their teacher through law and conscience. Transgression is sin. The proper response to sin is repentance and seeking forgiveness. The author of James and his readers have a common faith in "our glorious Lord Jesus Christ" (2:1), but none of the above understandings is disturbed.

There is no anti-matter dualism discernible in the epistle. The "world" (Jas 1:27), which is not to be "loved" (4:4), is the corrupting life of a pagan society. James is strong on prayer of petition in the Jewish manner, like Jesus (4:2f.). Equally Jewish, but un-Pauline, is the assumption that forgiveness of sins will come with the prayer of faith (5:15). The stern social teaching of the prophets appears here more than in any other NT book, accompanied by the apocalyptic threat of the destruction of money-oriented "flesh" by fire (5:1–6).

As to the concern of James with faith, works, and justification (Jas 2:14–25), the very vocabulary betrays a desire to oppose abuses of a teaching like Paul's that has come to his attention. In Paul, "works" always connotes boastfulness or a claim based on merit lodged before God. In James, the word means human deeds in an obedient (Abraham, v. 21) or compassionate (Rahab, v. 25) spirit. The author has no theory of works as a sign of faith or the fruits of faith; he does not explain how the two work together to achieve justification. His is a much simpler assumption. The two—religious disposition and good actions—have to exist together or else there is insincerity, faith without practice.

The brief discussion in James seems to be based on conceptions other than those of Paul. Ethical laxity was abroad in the church which was well worth opposing. Conceivably the confusion reflected in James was making headway and the genuine teaching of Paul very little progress. Interestingly, the phrase "by faith alone," which James denies is the principle of justification (Jas 2:24), is one Paul never uses, however much it is claimed he intended it. Thus, we have in James, not a clear contradiction of Pauline teaching, but a warning against what he seems to think is the common misconception that the justifying deed of God is independent of such matters as feeding and clothing the poor. James does not say how faith and works are to be related but only that they must be.

Paul, precisely by his silence at crucial points, has left himself open to the interpretation that the greatest deed of God with respect to us need have no discernible ethical consequence, indeed that any human works serve to impugn the divine act of justification. James's "faith" does not mean the same thing as Paul's. But James makes it perfectly clear that faith is something that must have tangible proof. One maintains at one's peril that such is not also the case in Paul.

The epistle of Jude is a warning to Christians to protect themselves against licentious persons who by their antinomian behavior create division. The language is apocalyptic, incorporating a Jewish favorite of the period, Enoch (Jude 14). It assumes an extensive angelology, as do other post-Maccabean writings. The writer holds that Michael, who disputed with the devil over Moses' body, was more reserved in his judgment on the devil than some contemporary revilers (Jude 9f.; the account is taken from the apocryphal Assumption of Moses). The chief thing to be said of this masterpiece of obloquy against moral deviants (Jude 1–3 and 20–22, 24–25, provide a welcome exception) is that its Christian author is fully familiar with Jewish apocalyptic literature. Toward the end of the twenty-five verses that make up the epistle he turns surprisingly gentle: "But you, beloved, grow strong in your holy faith through prayer in the Holy Spirit. Persevere in God's love and welcome the mercy of our Lord Jesus Christ which leads to life eternal" (Jude 20f.).

The epistle known as 2 Peter almost certainly derives from

Jude, even though the only phrases the two have verbally in common are Jude 13*b* and 2 Pt 2:17*b*. Other correspondence in content are Jude 4–16 and 2 Pt 2:1–18; Jude 17f. and 2 Pt 3:1–3; Jude 1f., 3, 5, 24, 25 and 2 Pt 1:1f., 5, 12; 3:14, 18. Jude is the harsher letter, 2 Peter the more elaborate and wordy (also the more sensitive to the Hebrew canon and the sequence of quotations from its books). Like the author of Jude, the author of 2 Peter is alive to the problem of liberty and law. He reminds his readers, as he exhorts them to virtue, of the "teaching of the holy prophets" and the "new command of the Lord and Savior preached to you by the apostles" (2 Pt 3:2).

JOHN'S TWO-LEVEL UNIVERSE

In the Johannine literature, the problems created by it with respect to a dualist world outlook are well known. The language is gnostic-tinged, even though both the Johannine gospel and epistles contain strong affirmations of Jesus' having truly come "in the flesh." Bultmann, challenged to produce his evidence for a pre-Christian gnostic redeemer myth, pointed to the fourth gospel. Indeed, one finds there two distinct levels or spheres, the "above" and the "below." Jesus comes "down" from heaven and will go back to the "place where he was before." He is lifted up from earth so as to draw all things to himself. He is not "of this world," just as his friends are not "of the world." No one can see the reign of God, says Jesus, unless he is begotten "again" or "from above"—the word employed means both. "Flesh begets flesh, spirit begets spirit" (Jn 3:6). "The light came into the world, but men loved darkness rather than light" (v. 19). "He who acts in truth comes into the light" (v. 21).

"No one can lay hold on anything," says John the Baptizer, "unless it is given him from on high" (Jn 3:27). Jesus comes from above and is above all; he testifies to what he has seen and heard (vv. 31, 32). The water he gives becomes a fountain within, leaping up to provide eternal life (4:14). "God is spirit, and those who worship him must worship in spirit and in truth" (v. 24). Jesus is characteristically "the son" in the fourth gospel, while God is "the Father." Just as the Father is a life-giver, so is the son (5:21). Faith in the God who sent Jesus gives eternal life; it assures a passage from death to life (v. 24).

The fourth gospel is marked by a vocabulary of seeing, knowing, abiding or dwelling in, believing. Jesus is the revealer of God throughout, on a mission to the world. "I tell you what I have seen in the Father's presence" (Jn 8:38), "the truth which I have heard from God" (v. 40). "While I am in the world I am the light of the world" (9:5).

Probably no other NT document has been as influential as John in creating a two-sphere universe: the earthly and the heavenly, the here and the hereafter, the seen and the unseen (which, as divine, is "genuine" or "true"). What happened to the teacher Jesus will happen to his friends. "No slave is greater than his master" (Jn 15:20). "If you belonged to the world, it would love you as its own; the reason it hates you is that you do not belong to the world. But I chose you out of the world" (v. 19). "The prince of this world has been condemned" (16:11). Throughout, the Johannine world is that demonic and human life which is set against God, not the universe or the earth of his creation. The terminology is clearly proper to apocalyptic Judaism. It was undoubtedly satisfactory to those familiar with the first centuries before and of the Christian era. It also explains why John was the darling of the early Gnostics.

It was important to Christianity that the categories of the fourth gospel could all be translated from the gnostic-tinged Hellenist Judaism of their birth—so close to the world of Qumrân—into the Platonic categories familiar to Alexandria and Athens. This was the thought world of the Greek fathers however vociferously they repudiated it.

What Paul calls "grace" John calls "truth," "life," "light." It is the same newness that both proclaim, the same succes-

sion of what was by what is. It was all God's gracious doing
and it left the way open to new dimensions of human life.
Again, we have an eon pattern of thought. There is futurist
eschatology in John in every passage where the eschaton is
interpreted as a reality of now, but the futurism is submerged
by the claim for the present. The world has been made over.
God dwells in it anew. He abides where his word is spoken
and believed in through his son. The creation is real and true
but in a new way—namely, by being shot through with deity
which has lately become present in it in Jesus, "the son." The
world of humanity has been saved, not judged or condemned, if the word of life spoken to it is heeded.

This means that interpretation of the fourth gospel can go
either way, in the gnostic dualist direction through being
read as a document of gnostic or Greek philosophy, or in the
incarnational monist direction if it is recognized as Jewish
wisdom thought. The latter will be the case if it is read for
what it is, a Christian and not a sectarian document. "Christian" here means Hellenist Jewish with Jesus Christ as the
specific difference, hence not halakic, spiritualist, or gnostic.
It means believing that God continues to be gracious in covenant love to the Jews of his special election, to whom gentiles
are joined in a prophesied outbreaking of that love.

THE LAW AND THE INCARNATE WORD

The fourth gospel poses the problem throughout of how
the things that have happened through Jesus Christ are
related to what has gone before. It is a document largely
unfriendly to "the Jews" but fully committed to "Israel."
C. K. Barrett writes: "The fact is that this gospel contains
Judaism, non-Judaism, and anti-Judaism. . . . John is both
Jewish and anti-Jewish."[6] The various symbolisms in John see
Jesus as the antitype or fulfillment of Moses, the manna, the
temple and temple mount, and even the divine name (the
tetragrammaton YHWH). First, however, comes the early

juxtaposition of "the Law that was given through Moses" and "grace and truth through Jesus Christ" (Jn 1:17).

The latter phrase occurs only here and in vv. 14 and 16 in the same chapter. This coupling in the prologue is frequently understood to be a rendering of the Bible's "loving-kindness and fidelity" (Jos 2:14; 2 Sm 2:6; 15:20; Ps 85:11). In the Septuagint, however, the two words are never rendered as in John's prologue but most often by words for mercy and truth. In Septuagintal practice the Hebrew word *ḥesed* is usually translated *'eleos* in Greek ("mercy," "loving-kind-ness"), while *ḥen* corresponds most often to *charis* ("grace," "favor").

One finds that a view such as the following occurs frequently in Christian writing: "The programmatic statement of the fourth evangelist, 'The law was given through Moses; grace and truth came through Jesus Christ' (1:17), could just as well come from Paul, and might be used equally as well as the Pauline statements for defining the relationship of law and gospel."[7] However, the apparent Pauline antithesis between law and grace is not to be found in John's prologue, and commentators are unwise to assume its presence there.[8] While the two NT authors use the word for grace in the generic sense of "gift," with Paul it is the gift of salvation whereas John sees it as the gift of truth fully present in God's son. Paul's grace is a soteriological reality bound to the cross, John's the eschatological revelation bound to the incarnation of the word. The Law is a gift for John, something "given" (Jn 1:17). He needs another word for what takes place in Jesus. Forgoing the normal words for "gift," he turns to *charis*, "gracious gift" or "grace."

A hendiadys is not the same as a couplet but is a figure of speech that conveys a single idea through two nouns, one of them having the force of an adjective. In John's usage the substantive is "truth" understood as God's revelation in Christ. It is more, it is "gracious truth." "The gift of revela-tion" would be another way to render the phrase.[9] The glory "as of an only son" which the evangelist says "we have seen"

(Jn 1:14) refers to God's dwelling in our midst as a man. That son is the "word become flesh" of the same verse, "full of the grace of truth." The overall balance is between the gift of the Law and another objective gift of God in Jesus Christ (v. 17); hence "grace and truth" are in no case subjective states in God. The "enfleshed word" is filled with "gracious truth" (v. 14) in the sense that with the one comes the other. Jesus Christ is that truth graciously given.

Believers in Jesus Christ share in this "glory" (v. 14) or "fullness" (v. 16). One revelation has been substituted for another, v. 16 being best translated "gift in place of gift."[10] One objective teaching of God replaces another, which was itself a gift. The contrast is precisely this: whereas the Law was given *through* Moses, the grace of truth *in* Jesus Christ (v. 17) is none other than his person. As "only son" turned toward the innermost self of the Father, he *"was* the revelation" (v. 18). That last phrase seems to render the Greek better than the usual insertion of an object in English: "he revealed him" (viz., Jesus revealed God). The verb is consciously intransitive and echoes the phrase in v. 14 which identifies the only son of the Father with the fullness of the grace of truth.

Thus we have an early indication in John's gospel of the author's conviction that God has given a gift through Moses —the Law—and added or supplied in place of it a revelation more gracious still. The difference is constituted by the words that denote a "fullness" in Jesus Christ, an adjective in v. 14 and a noun in v. 16. A revelation once given through a law is now transmitted fully as a person.

The symbolism of the fourth gospel is its very warp and woof. Yet so multivalent is it that one hesitates to isolate motifs and expound their meaning with certainty. The prologue insists so frequently that in the person of Jesus the fullness of revelation has come, that we cannot err in finding in Jesus the revealer of God. Thus, he is the "choice wine kept until now" (Jn 2:10), succeeding the water of ceremonial purification in the stone jars which are six, one less than seven. As the perfect vehicle of God's teaching to whom "the Father . . . has given everything over" (3:35), he can also be viewed as "living water" (4:10); a healer who is at work even as God is at work (cf. 5:17); a fountain of the spirit who will slake thirst once that spirit is given (cf. 7:37ff.). Since Moses wrote about Jesus, not to believe in him is not to accept the Lawgiver and vice versa (cf. 5:45ff.). Jesus is the real heavenly bread as contrasted with the manna of old (cf. 6:32–35). Belief in him means the continuing sustenance that leads to life (cf. v. 58), presumably in contrast to the teaching that Moses gave in the desert.

The charge in the fourth gospel that "none of you keeps [the Law of Moses]" (7:19) is embedded in some bitter words about hypocrisy. The embattled evangelist is maintaining against some contemporaries that Jesus—and presumably disciples like himself—unlike their opponents, seek God's glory and are not bent on self-glorification (see v. 18). This heated exchange does not inform us on the Christian attitude toward the Law except to say, in the spirit of the Jesus of the synoptics, that the Christians are more honest with respect to the Law's intent than some of its protagonists. The teaching of Jesus viewed as heavenly doctrine has evidently replaced the Mosaic precepts in the Johannine community.

One cannot conceive of this community's members as observants in anything like a Matthean sense. Yet there is recourse to the biblical requirement of at least two witnesses if any condemnatory judgment is to stand (Jn 8:13, 17; cf. Dt 17:6; 19:15; Nm 35:30). It is praiseworthy to be of Abraham's stock, but this does not necessarily bring with it to "those Jews who believed in him" (8:31) freedom from lies or murderous intent (see 8:33–59). The rabbinic conviction that God does not hear the prayers of impenitent sinners is also upheld (9:31; cf. Ps 66:16ff.; 109:7; Prv 15:29; Is 1:15). Finally, the fourth gospel is built squarely on the assumption that the Hebrew Scriptures are God's word ("and scripture cannot lose its force," 10:35), a word which Jesus fulfills. Biblical passages are seldom quoted directly but are employed allusively. This Johannine technique probably was the basis of certain opposition between the two parties of Jews, Christian and rabbinic. John cites the opponents in this way: "We are disciples of Moses. We know that God spoke to Moses, but we have no idea where this man comes from" (9:28f.). It is clear from this that Jesus was being preached by the evangelist and his circle in a way totally incomprehensible to a certain type of Jewish or Christian Jewish hearer.

COMMANDMENT IN JOHN

Commandment is an important concept in the fourth gospel. In the plural in the Septuagint it normally describes the totality of legal ordinances, while the singular can convey either a precept or the whole Law. In John the word describes the command that God gives to Christ about laying down his life (Jn 10:18) but also as regards what to say and how to speak (12:49f.; 14:31; 15:10, the latter in plural form and as Jesus' commandments to his friends, as well as the Father's to him). John uses the word to describe the precepts of Jesus, both in the singular to specify the new commandment of loving one another as he has loved his friends (13:34; 15:12) and in the plural, unspecified as to content (14:15, 21; 15:10*a*).

There is nothing unusual about John's use of this term to translate the Hebrew *mitzvah* and *mitzvoth*. The synoptics do this frequently (e.g., Mk 10:5; Lk 18:20). Later NT writings will use the word to speak of the whole Christian religion as "God's command" (1 Tm 6:14), the "holy law" (2 Pt 2:21), or the "command of the Lord and Savior [given] through your apostles" (2 Pt 3:2). What is peculiar to John is the assumption that on Jesus' lips the "commandment," whether in the singular or the plural, involves mutual love among the disciples like his for his friends which culminated in his death. Clearly, the whole revelation of God through Jesus has come down to that preserved in the Johannine circle, without being preceded by the command of the Shema to love God with all one's heart and soul and strength (cf. Dt 6:4).

The passage 1 Jn 4:7–21 mentions loving God in vv. 20 and 21. One can do so only because God took the initiative in loving us (vv. 9, 10, 11, 16). Again, the "love of God"—an objective genitive meaning love for him—is specified as a matter of keeping his commandments (5:2). These are spoken of as not burdensome (v. 3) but are not otherwise specified. It is doubtful that the Johannine believers had any understanding of fulfilling any precepts, biblical included, other than those of mutual charity based on Jesus' loving act of laying down his life.

In conclusion it can be said that biblical teaching on the Law in the Johannine circle did not survive in any form recognizable to Jews. The relentless polemic against "the Jews," and the saying of Jesus that God is spirit and all who worship him must do so in spirit and in truth (cf. Jn 4:24), prevailed. If Christianity has come to think of itself as organically unrelated to what went before in Jewish history, with believers little or not at all beholden to Israel's past, the Johannine writings must bear a large part of the burden. Any typology of continuity, however effective it may have been for a Jewish readership of John's time, comes as completely new knowledge to modern Christians. They cannot discern it unless aided by much exegetical assistance.

As to the gnostic character of Johannine concepts and language, we are wise to say—as with Paul's letters—that there can be a fully orthodox or a fully gnosticizing reading of the same materials.[11] The gospel and epistles of John are pro-matter in the hands of Ignatius, anti-matter as read by Heracleon. The church voted with the former in principle but has been much influenced by the latter in fact.

SUMMARY

The light shed on our problem by some of the catholic or general epistles and by the gospel and epistles of John is diverse. This much, at least, can be stated fairly:

—While eschatological considerations continued to pervade Christian teaching as the end of the first century approached, they were never such as to divert attention from the importance of this life or the responsible ethical choices that had to be made in the course of it.

—The churches had a full awareness that Christian existence was a life of faith in Jesus Christ, of love, in God the Father, and growth in grace (cf. Jude 1; 2 Pt 3:18). Yet they taught the necessity of good deeds, obedience to God's commands, and repentance, quite as though Jesus' role as savior (cf. 2 Pt 1:1; 2:20) had left those matters undisturbed.

—The Mosaic Law was being identified with the summary made of it under the titles "the perfect law of freedom" (Jas 1:25), "the kingly law" (Jas 2:8), "the command of the Lord and Savior preached to you by the apostles" (2 Pt 3:2), the "new commandment" (Jn 13:34; 15:12), and "the one we have had from the start" (2 Jn 5). This command, in the Johannine writings, consisted of the mutual love that prevailed among Jesus and his friends. Some churches seem to have let all other types of Law observance yield to this one.

—The existence of believers in Jesus Christ in the Johannine present was called "life" and "light" and was alone true or real before God. Jesus' presence in the midst of his friends, through the activity of another Paraclete he had sent from the Father, created this new existence.

—There was abroad in some churches confusion over the meaning of "faith" to the extent that possession of it was thought to absolve from the necessity of doing good deeds. But the notion of being saved apart from good deeds was as repugnant to Christianity as it was to the life of the Jews.

—In sum, although one eon of world history was thought by the authors to be over and another begun, the realities of the present life were not denied, only those of the present eon. In Jesus Christ the Law of Moses was made perfect with the fullness of God's fidelity, not abrogated—it had to be kept because it was the Torah of the beginning of the last days.

Chapter V

GRECO-ROMAN
INFLUENCES

It seems fair to describe Christianity as a Hellenized version of the religion of Israel with some important new features. The trend toward Hellenization in the Jewish community was reversed by the efforts of Johanan ben Zakkai and the rabbis. Jewish thinkers of today tend to say that the trend went on apace in the new religion, culminating in the veneration of the man Jesus as a god-hero alongside God. But, of course, the Greco-Roman influence on the Jewish group that became the Christian church was more complex than that. It was in the NT period a much smaller influence and in the period after A.D. 175 a much greater one than is commonly realized. The latter is a fact even for those who consider themselves "Bible Christians" or committed to the Bible alone as their principle of faith. This chapter needs to explore the lasting impression made on the apostolic teaching by the Greco-Roman world, especially in the matters of grace and free will and an optimistic or a pessimistic view of the world and human nature.

It is commonly said that Christianity was deeply influenced by the mystery religions of the Greco-Roman world.[1] However, we have little written documentation on these religions. Most of what we have consists of inscriptions and excavated sanctuaries. The chief exception is the account of the induction into the mysteries of Isis found in *The Golden Ass* (or *Metamorphoses*) of Apuleius.[2] Apart from this, there are the positions taken by the Greek Christian apologists who cite similarities between Christian and pagan religious practice, only to underscore the sublimity of their own and the absurdity of the other. They do this at times in a triumphal spirit, claiming that all that the pagans do the Christians do better and with some real effect. God's activity in Christ and the Holy Spirit, they maintain, makes the difference between meaningful and meaningless signs, between miracle and magic.

Jewish and Christian scholars unsympathetic to the concept of outward signs of saving faith have produced a sizable literature establishing the syncretic character of the earliest Christian symbols. Obviously the data of the NT and sub-apostolic era employed by these scholars can be read two ways: as regrettable departures respectively from rabbinic teaching and the Pauline teaching on faith; or as ingenious accommodations to the Greco-Roman world in which the Jewish teaching about Jesus was gaining strength.

Arthur Nock and A. J. Festugière[3] have examined the change of outlook of initiates into the mystery cults of the ancient world, as reported in pagan sources. Few though the sources are, they provide evidence of a thoroughly new existence for the devotees. The cults had this conviction in common with the Pauline concept of new life "in Christ" or the Johannine transition to "life" or "light" as something realized in the present. Neither scholar posits the fairly direct dependence of Christianity on the mystery religions suggested by the history-of-religions school as represented by Reitzenstein, Bousset, Bultmann, Bartsch, and others. The latter are much at home in second-century gnostic patterns of thought. They assume a full-blown, pre-Christian gnosis—complete with redeemer myth—on which early Christianity drew. A discussion of this view, fairly conventional in the world of scholarship, will appear later in this chapter.[4] At this point an inquiry into the place of humanity in the material world in Greek and Latin sources seems to be a useful place to start.

The reader is warned to look for elements of mystical identification and exhilaration, together with the near-total absence of conformity to law as an element of religious identity.

PESSIMISM IN THE GRECO-ROMAN WORLD

A common assumption is that early Christianity, beginning
in the NT, was infected by a metaphysical dualism acquired
from Hellenist Judaism, which in turn was Iranian in origin.
A somewhat different line, however, is taken by Eric R.
Dodds in his *Pagan and Christian in an Age of Anxiety*.[5]
Dodds looks into certain aspects of religious experience in
the period between Marcus Aurelius' accession to the throne
(A.D. 161) and the death of Constantine (A.D. 337). The author
records much of the pre-Christian Greek philosophical
thought that preceded Marcus Aurelius. Thus he gives us the
assumptions prevailing in the gentile world where the gospel
was first preached. Dodds likewise develops these assumptions in the form that served as the matrix for the second- and
third-century beginnings of Christian theology. A self-con-
fessed agnostic, he nevertheless fails to see Christianity as a
"barbarian theosophy," in Proclus' term, that blotted out the
sunshine of Hellenism. He is, rather, inclined to discover in
pagan sources a widespread moral and intellectual insecurity
to which Christianity offered an answer.

There was a view of the cosmos, going back to Aristotle and
the Greek astronomers, which held that the earth was dense
and impure compared with the spheres of the moon, the sun,
and the five planets. This meant that the earth was mean and
poor in contrast to the celestial spheres, especially the eighth
or empyrean heaven consisting of fire or light. No Christian,
working in a biblical context of the divine creation of all
things, actively challenged this conception until the sixth
century.[6] The tininess and insignificance of the planet earth
was noted by many of the ancients. Cicero, Seneca, Celsus,
and Lucian moralized from this fact on the vanity of human

desires. The world of antiquity had numerous passages depicting the flight of the soul through the universe, whether in death or contemplation, thereby escaping from the illusory to the real. It remained for Marcus Aurelius to cap the thought of Seneca and Plutarch concerning the earth as a tiny point in space. All three viewed man's life as a brief instant in time separating two eternities. This is far from the biblical view of things.

In any search for the pre-Christian roots of an adverse view of the world and matter, we have to look behind Greek philosophy. In general, the thought of Plato, Aristotle, and the later Stoics could not condemn the cosmos outright. The last named had no scheme of transcendent otherness. Even Plato's thought featured a visible cosmos dependent upon rather than opposed to a world of ideas or forms. Platonism was a dualism, to be sure, but the world was not thought an unmitigated evil in respect to an invisible good. Plato concluded his discourse on the nature of the universe by praising it as an image of the intelligible, a perceptible god, "the greatest, best, fairest, most perfect," alone of its kind and one.[7] "The creator was good and the good can never be jealous of anything. . . . God desired that all things should be good and nothing bad, so far as this was attainable."[8] This is not the language of a person who scorned the material world. Still, it continues to be a subject for debate how much Plato looked upon matter as the cause of evil.

There was in Greek thought a dualism more radical than Plato's, but its roots must be sought farther east. The pagans were not without a concept of matter as a principle independent of God, not created by him and resistant to his will. Its origins are attributed variously to Plato and Pythagoras; it is most developed by the Neo-Pythagorean Numenius. This Greek dualism ran counter to the main tradition, which always acknowledged some measure of form and light in the cosmos. Greek thought, while it was tinged slightly by Eastern metaphysical dualism, never capitulated to it thoroughly. A distinction must be made between the practical pessimism of Greek thought about the world, the result of its moderate dualism, and the absolute pessimism that marked gnostic and Hermetic thought, influenced by the modified dualism of Persia turned absolute.

In Persian belief the world was the theater of conflict between Ormazd and Ahriman, the principles of Good and Evil. This differs from later gnostic and Hermetic thought which will give this world over to darkness completely. Even 1 John tends in the latter direction when its author says: "We know that we are of God, and the whole world lies in the evil one" (1 Jn 5:19). This conception of the world as a totality of evil made the second-century Christian gnostics deny that God had made it. They were not followed in this by orthodox Christians who resisted Marcion's rejection of the Jewish Scriptures and their creator God, holding instead for the goodness of the world and the God who was its maker.

SATAN'S CHANGING ROLE IN THE BIBLE

Practically speaking, the Bible of the Jews holds what has been called a relaxed monism with respect to creatures. It has no spirit-matter duality, only an ethical opposition between disobedient creatures condemned to evil and the great majority subjected to testing who are good. Satan appears in the later Jewish Scriptures (in three places only: 1 Chr 21:1; Jb 1:6; Zec 3:1) as an emissary from the heavenly court to incite and accuse people and test their fidelity to God. He develops from this into God's adversary ("by the envy of the devil, death entered the world," Wis Sol 2:24) and in apocryphal writing as the prince of darkness and ruler of evil powers. This new role sees him slipping into the Garden of Eden as the serpent, becoming instrumental in the origins of human evil or the fall. John's gospel reflects the tendency: "He brought death to man from the beginning. . . . He is a liar and the father of lies" (Jn 8:44). Jewish literature comes to have fantastic stories about his disguising himself or becoming the vehicle of the evil spirit Sammael so as to take Eve unawares.[9]

The dualistic tendency in Zoroastrian religion may have been influential in this development. People experience the struggle of good and evil within themselves. It is not hard to extrapolate from this internal reality to the cosmic scene. The Jewish conviction that God was in control of the world led to the rejection of absolute dualism.[10] The next step was the view that the evil powers were originally good but fell in an act of rebellion. They continually test their strength against God's, even though they will ultimately be defeated by him. Paul has "the god of this world" blinding the thoughts of unbelievers (2 Cor 4:4), while in Luke's account of the temptation of Jesus the devil offered him "all this authority and their glory, for it has been delivered to me, and I give it to whomever I wish" (Lk 4:6; Mt 4:8 is not so sweeping in its claim for diabolic power). These Christian texts are consonant with post-biblical Jewish thought on the devil, God's adversary.

WAS THERE A PRE-CHRISTIAN GNOSTICISM?

The evidence does not seem to support that there was a full-scale pre-Christian gnostic system, nor even a satisfactory theory of "sectarian Jewish origins" for the movement. There was, rather, a widespread tendency toward metaphysical dualism abroad in the Persian, Hellenist, and Jewish worlds of Paul's time. A century and a half later these tendencies appear fully clothed in mythological dress in the Christian gnostic systems and in Jewish mysticism. Dualism emerged in the various structured gnosticisms nourished by philosophy as much as by religion.

The easiest explanation of how a modified dualism entered into Jewish life after the exile is that the thinkers of this period were influenced by Zoroastrians while in Babylon. No less an authority than R. C. Zaehner describes the Jewish

exiles in Babylonia as "thoroughly impregnated with Zoroastrian ideas." From them these ideas found their way into
Christianity also.[11] He may be right, but like all who theorize
in this way he must take a known proximity of ideas in place
and time as identical with a causal relation. It is just as likely
that both Zoroastrian and Jewish thought are responses to
the common problems of evil and pain in the ancient world
of which Jews and Persians were a part. The book of Job was
one attempted Jewish solution, and the modified Jewish dualism in which the LORD and Satan struggled for the mastery
in a good world flawed by evil is another. The Persians, un-
affected by a strong conception of a God who created all and
found it good, gravitated toward a creator God of all that *was*
good. They opposed to him a lesser deity who acted as a
spoiler or destroyer from outside the good creation in which
he had no part.[12]

The origins of the spirit of self-imposed disciplines of hardship among Christians is a mystery. Feats of fasting and other
bodily rigors are told of the earliest monks. There is nothing
biblical about the practice. Jesus' word about castration was
probably spoken in praise of chastity in the hyperbolic mold
of plucking out the eye and cutting off the hand (cf. Mt 5:29).
The important question to ask is, What was the psychological
condition of the Christian community that it should have
been so violent in its opposition to second marriage, and so
enthusiastic for total sexual abstention?[13] Its literal and undoubtedly erroneous interpretation of 1 Tm 3:2 and Ti 1:6 as
forbidding a second marriage to the clergy is a case in point.
Paul was quite relaxed over the marriage of anyone "free of
a wife" (1 Cor 7:28). The eschatological hope may have been
influential on Paul, with his "shape of this world passing
away" (v. 31), but it lost its grip on the non-Jewish Christians
who predominated in the church after A.D. 135. There is no
evidence that the tendency had its roots in the Hellenic
tradition, any more than it could have derived from the
Jewish attitudes on sex, which were generally affirmative.
Nor will it do to resort immediately to Iranian dualism for an

explanation, as if everything anti-this-worldly had to originate in Persia. That kind of thinking can be a convenient catchall for our ignorance of the facts.

ANCIENT WEARINESS WITH LIFE

A better explanation may be sought in the nearly universal weariness with life that gripped the ancient world at the time Christianity was coming to birth. For many and sufficient reasons the culture grew anxious and nervous: there were barbarian invasions, disease, inflation, war. The people engaged in massive self-examination, self-reproach, and self-punishment. There was a certain amount of self-inflicted mutilation and much suicide. This hatred of the self and of the body made its inroads into the philosophical schools, which were limited of course in their numerical influence. Its greatest victories occurred in gnostic-oriented salvationist religions. The church, insisting that all of life save sin is good, identified these sects and parties as having no share in its Hebrew heritage. Consequently the various gnosticisms, the religion of the Encratites, of Marcion and Montanus were declared heretical by the church fathers.

But the church was at the same time deeply infected by the very forces it resisted. The wonder is, not that it was influenced, but that it was influenced so little, since it dwelt largely in a culture under Greco-Roman influence even in Egypt, Syria, Mesopotamia, and Persia. The salutary influence of Jewish thought was minimized by the practical absence of Jews from Christian life. The goodness of human life and the world found its witness in silent books, not in a living community of persons.

The religious manifestations of the gnostic redemption drama (plus the spiritualist enthusiasm of 1 and 2 Corinthians, and the "myths and fables" of Colossians, the Pastorals, 1 John, Jude, and 2 Peter) were vigorously opposed in the first century. This opposition appeared within and outside the Christian movement, in ways that have to be thought of as basically independent of one another. The common element is a religious syncretism, in which oriental mythology —non-Jewish fused with Jewish—is mixed with Greek philosophy.

The profoundest insight into the phenomenon is not that of the history-of-religions school, which tends to see in it a single fairly coherent system manifested in many places. Rather, it seems to have been a philosophically undergirded myth that served as a vehicle for a new understanding of the cosmos and the self by the late classical world.

A distinction must be made between dualistic conceptions of the universe that rely on gnosis for human deliverance and full-scale gnostic schemes of redemption which feature a hero who is divine or semi-divine.[14] Thus, in the Jewish apocalyptic literature, Philo, the Qumrân scrolls, and the book of Wisdom there are found ideas that should be called pre-gnostic, or gnostic in tendency. The distinguishing characteristics are a devaluation of the present age and a trust in the age to come, which is not just a succeeding epoch on earth but a world somehow above. Only in the first century, inchoately, and in complete form in the second, does there appear a gnosticism properly so called. It exists at the edges of Judaism and Christianity. Yet it does not hesitate to put itself forward as authentic Christianity because its thorough spiritualism is superior to the prevailing form.

The gnostic expositors within Christian circles interpreted every NT passage that favored their outlook (and they found many) in ways that showed the superiority of the pneumatic to the psychic, the mature or "perfect" to babes, light and life to death and darkness. Were it not for the commitment of Paul and the synoptic evangelists to the reality of Jesus' manhood and his death, and of John to his being in the flesh, they might have had the best of it. Those realistic features of NT teaching were seized on by 1 Clement, Ignatius, Polycarp, and the author of the letter To Diognetus. Among them they made a case for Christianity as anything but a flight from earthly realities. The gnostic challenge was met and put down, in one sense resoundingly but in another sense barely.

Summary

The following things seem sure about the Greco-Roman world into which Christianity came:

—Christianity came to birth in a tired world that looked for grandiose schemes of knowledge rather than a struggle on this world's terms. Its first appeal was to Jews and God-fearers and proselytes, then to Greeks, among whom there were some with philosophic training. These were free spirits who knew that God had acted first on their behalf and that they had only to act in response.

—As the waves of war and want and psychic insecurity battered harder and as Christianity got farther away from its Jewish way of looking at life and the world, believers turned more and more to the spiritualist categories from which they had been rescued.

—They looked longingly at a reading of salvation in Christ which saw them as all but powerless and God as the all-powerful savior, his gift of creation and nature a doubtful one, his grace—understood as something more or different from the creation—its only remedy.

—The Christians of this later age, the second and third centuries, sought scapegoats for their undoubted adversities in the weak and wounded condition of human nature, in evil spirits pitted against them, in the shortcomings of familiar matter in comparison to pure spirit, the attractive unknown.

—They imposed non-biblical understandings on a variety of places in the Bible, chiefly by the literal understanding of their own mythic literature.

—The result of all this was a departure from the spirit of the Hebrew Scriptures and that of Jesus in such matters as the goodness of life and the power of human choice, even while the general metaphysical understandings of the Bible and the NT were kept.

Chapter VI

THE CHURCH FATHERS
SET THE COURSE

The fathers of the church had but one desire: to transmit biblical faith in the form in which they found it. To do so was, of course, impossible. Every age and culture puts its stamp on a revelation that was itself culturally conditioned. We cannot know how the teachings of the NT on grace and nature or on law and faith reach us unless we see how the church fathers read both testaments of Scripture. It was upon their interpretations that the great medieval doctors and the Reformers built. This chapter will therefore explore the patristic era somewhat as a necessary condition of understanding the faith we now hold.

The Greek fathers of the church viewed all of God's acts as grace, whether of creation, providence, or redemption. Father, Son, and Spirit have a part in each divine action. As Gregory of Palamas expressed it in the fourteenth century, God gives himself to creatures through his energies, not through participation in his essence. But the share in the divine reality is real. The self-giving accomplished in Christ may even be called a divinization of humanity. The individual human being is free to take in the gift of God according to capacity.

The initial, graced condition of the race was not viewed as sufficient, however, to see people through the course of life. Sin did some damage to the freedom of the will without destroying it. The redemption worked by Christ was potentially the gift of all. It became actual to the individual at baptism. According to Greek patristic thought, weakened human powers were restored in Christ to a higher level than Adam's. The church was the place where growth in grace was accomplished. Humanity has a natural inclination toward the good. Each person is free to choose. Each can and must change from potential sinner to saint. This is achieved by the prompting of God, who does not, however, destroy human freedom in enlarging humanity's capacity for good. Clearly this doctrine, so close to that of the Hebrew Bible, views human nature as more robust than is allowed by the Augustinian development that became the heritage of the West.

The pagan Greeks had taught that "destiny," "chance," and "fate" were irresistible forces. Added to them, in the popular mind, were the inscrutable wills of the gods and the plotting of human life written in the stars. Against this popular fear, stoic philosophy set the concept of the divine will. It was not entirely successful in preserving the freedom of the human will. Socrates had featured free will and the possibility of overcoming sin by knowledge and right motives. But this teaching had not taken hold of the popular mind as had the ineluctability of fate. It was this spirit of helplessness that the early Christian teachers opposed with their commitment to human free will, whether for good or evil.[1] God foreknew how humanity would choose and he did not interfere. Having made this creature free, he respected his own decision.[2] He would reward and punish according to the way freedom was used. Origen has a passage in his treatise *Against Celsus* in which he says that providence operates in accordance with individual free will which, "insofar as possible, is always being led on to be better. . . . The nature of our free will is to admit various possibilities."[3] And Tatian writes: "It is our free will that has ruined us. We were free but we have become slaves; for our sins were we sold."[4] Gnostic theories entered the Christian stream as a dizzying variety of heresies far more committed to the human necessity of sinning than any Greek philosophy or Roman religion. In contrast with gnostic schemes of "original sin," the early Greek fathers up to and including Irenaeus had no such doctrine. Gnosticism based its theories of redemption on the supposition that humanity was fated to wrongdoing as part of a larger necessity. Predetermination ruled all humanity, the "carnals" and the "psychics" inevitably and the "spirituals" if they failed to conform to gnostic redemptive patterns. Humanity was a nutshell on the raging billows of a sea it could not control. Sin could not be avoided. Only gnostic "grace"—frequently independent of ethical considerations—would bring salvation.

In the face of this challenge it is not surprising that Christian teachers should have responded with a strong affirmation of self-determing human freedom, a divine gift. Irenaeus is forthright about this:

> Those who have apostatized from the light given by the Father and transgressed the law of liberty have done so through their own fault, since they have been created free agents and possessed of power over themselves.[5]

GRACE, GOD'S ENABLING GIFT

In the apostolic fathers and their contemporaries (The Didache, 1 Clement, Ignatius of Antioch, Polycarp, Pseudo-Barnabas, Hermas, 2 Clement), grace was God's gift enabling an obedient response to the call to a new life. This fact has traditionally been deplored by Christian theologians, especially of the Reformation, for whom Paul's teaching on grace and law and John's on light and life are taken as normative. The writers of the later part of the first and the early part of the second century interpreted the gospel "in terms of Judaistic tenor."[6] Jewish concern with the Law and the use of the Septuagint as the inspired scripture of the church are named as the positive contributing factors. The post-apostolic church had as its primary divine sanction the Jewish one, "You will be judged by your works." Paul had presumably set the church free from this norm with his teaching that God had set humanity right with him. For him, fulfillment of "works of the Law" was no longer a standard for judgment. Paul's letters, although in circulation, not only were not yet "canon" (as indeed the gospels were not) but had not achieved the normative status they were later to enjoy.

In any case, it is a commonplace in modern theology—Protestant more than Catholic and Orthodox—to speak of the gospel as placed in opposition to pagan myths and mores by the apostolic fathers. They were said to interpret the gospel as a new law. The implication is that the cure is little better than the disease. In principle there was no change from the Jewish legal outlook—even when the substance of the ethical teaching was taken from the sayings of Jesus in the gospels. The Pauline teaching on grace is largely absent in this period.

The second-century writers are sometimes chastised for striving to shape their lives according to the new way, relying on grace as an enabling power which worked on an *ad hoc* basis. They favored repentance, to be sure, just as the Jews had done, as self-amendment before God adequate to secure his pardon and mercy. Hellenism was identified as the chief formative factor in this development. By contrast Paul's pure gospel, which derived from neither Judaism nor Hellenism, proved attractive to neither Jew nor Greek at the start. The result was an early gospel of moralism, not of God's saving deed. Irenaeus (fl. ca. 180) delivered the church from this situation with his restoration of Paul's epistles. Despite this service, "some of the implications of the gospel, grace particularly, were never recovered till the Reformation."[7]

This narrow, if widespread, interpretation of the teaching of the apostolic fathers should not keep us from making a few observations on their genuine achievements. They regarded grace as a divine aid in the struggle to obey the new law of the gospel. They associated grace with the Spirit, understood as the divine energy contributing to a beauty, truth, and sanctification which overcame the power of evil. They saw grace as the spiritual power which made the believer god-like. It resided in the church, which could dispense it through certain acts such as sacraments. Of these, the bishop was the custodian in the local church after the time of Ignatius of Antioch (d. ca. 110).

It is easy to see these tendencies as a total misconstruing of the new gospel of faith in the redeeming death of Christ. The Reformers so viewed them. The ancient churches of Alexandria and Edessa, of Greece and Rome, however, did not. They thought that the synthesis of new and old achieved in the second century had divine significance. One clear achievement of the writers known as apologists, beginning with Justin Martyr (d. ca. 165), was to root the gospel in the Hebrew Scriptures and link it with a respect for the processes of human thought. The Greek-speaking writers of 150 and following viewed Jesus as the teacher of a philosophy that could and should be adhered to. Model, pedagogue, and fulfiller of every biblical foreshadowing, Jesus had to be obeyed if anyone was to be saved by God.

A CENTURY WITHOUT A THEORY OF A FALL

It is both interesting and important to observe that there is no reference to a theory of a fall in Adam in Greek Christian literature before the writings of Justin. Only the Epistle of Barnabas (a pseudonymous attribution, ca. 130) refers to a primordial individual sin "through the serpent." The writer sets up a brief parallel between the snakes that caused death in the desert as a result of the Israelites' transgression and "the transgression [that] was wrought in Eve through the snake."[8] Clement of Rome has no such reference. It is equally absent from The Didache, the epistles of Ignatius and Polycarp, and the Apology of Aristides. Contemporaneous with Barnabas' reference to Exodus and Gn 3 as the explanation of sin and death are two others, one canonical and one extracanonical, which follow different paths.

2 Peter (ca. 130) was probably opting for the theory of angelic lust for intercourse with women (Gn 6:4) to account for the presence of evil in humanity: "Through knowledge of him who has called us through his own glory and power . . . you who have fled a world corrupted by lust may become sharers of the divine nature" (2 Pt 1:3f.). "Did God spare even the angels who sinned? He did not! He held them captive in Tartarus—consigned them to pits of darkness, to be guarded until judgment" (2:4). The context of the latter passage is not disobedience, but lust and greed (see vv. 6, 10, 14, 18). This theory of angelic Watchers (the "wakeful") as the originators of human evil is predominant in post-biblical Jewish literature.

Hermas' Shepherd—a work composed at some undetermined period between 90 and 140—features the Jewish theory of the origin of sin that identifies the evil impulse and the good impulse as two tendencies implanted in each soul by God at birth.[9] "If you set it before yourself that [these commandments] can be kept you will easily keep them, and they will not be difficult; but if it already comes into your heart that they can not be kept by man, you will not keep them."[10]

THE FALL IN THE APOLOGISTS

Christian unconcern with the sin of Adam (or Eve, in Barnabas; cf. Wis Sol 2:24) comes to an end in the middle of the second century. The apologists Justin, Tatian, and Theophilus of Antioch teach the doctrine of a fall in Adam. This is surprising in the light of the total silence of nearly a century on the matter, since the death of Paul. Justin in his *Dialogue with Trypho,* having developed the Barnabas parallel,[11] states that the whole race is under a curse as a result of its sins.[12] He sets the death of the human race ever since the serpent deceived Adam in juxtaposition with the responsibility of individuals for their sins, without establishing any cause-effect relation between the two.[13] He does, however, claim that redemption in Christ is the counterpart of the fall[14] and sets up a parallel between the virgin Eve (who begets disobedience and death) and the virgin Mary (who says in faith and joy, "Be it done"). This parallel Irenaeus will develop at length, in extension of Paul's Christ-Adam figure.[15]

None of the second-century thinkers has a doctrine of original sin as it was later developed. All assume, on the basis of the Genesis account (Gn 3), some condemnation of the race as a result of sin, and some relation between death and sin. For them, Satan is the chief malefactor, not Adam. He drives Cain to murder, and through Cain's sin (not Adam's, whose repentance kept Satan from killing him), death entered the world. Death then spread to all members of the human race.[16] What is important about Justin, Tatian, and Theophilus is that they framed their theories on the origin of evil —fuzzy enough in each case—in terms of the demonism prevailing in Palestine and Syria. While aware of Paul's Adam-Christ parallel illustrating Jesus' status as firstborn of the just, they gravitated toward a serpent theme rather than toward any theory of hereditary sin and guilt.

Basic to the apologists' conception of the devil as spoiler rather than the first man was the conviction that the creation had received in Christ an "implanted grace of the gift of the spirit"[17] and that grace upheld the prophets in time of persecution.[18] The "implanted word" was at work among the pagans for Justin,[19] even as the holy spirit had spoken through such ministers of grace as Noah and Jonah.[20] The subsequent Greek fathers would never lose sight of this conviction that everything in the world was a manifestation of the power of grace. Thus, Basil could write in the fourth century that "all good coming down on us from divine power" was a working of that grace which produces everything in all."[21] The beginnings of human life came with the grace of God's inbreathing,[22] which was in turn a share in the wisdom and truth of the divine word.[23] Everywhere there is grace and all is grace.

Paul's Writing Becomes Scripture

The early spirit of the affirmation of human powers could not have yielded to the Adamic fall doctrine as abruptly as it did after A.D. 150 without some cause. Undoubtedly that cause was the canonization of Paul's writings, which hitherto had been letters to young churches. This gave oracular force to the Adam story to account for death and sin, over both the angelic lust tale of Gn 6 and the evil impulse theory of Judaism. The garden narrative—which Paul did not feature in its details—was no longer an interesting bit of biblical typology, a useful illustration, but an oracle of God in a new sense. It was now *the* explanation of how sin entered the world. Up until this late-second-century shift, the pervasive influence of spirits who had become evil by refusing to serve God had prevailed.

Although a difference set in with the widespread acceptance of Paul's epistles as Scripture, the biblical source on the origins of evil continued for some time to be early Genesis stories taken globally. Adam and Eve come before Cain and the three sons of Noah, but all are implicated equally in the history of sin. These tales come at the beginning of the human story, which is also the story of God's design to save. All the characters in the tales are responsible for human sinfulness, not the earliest pair only; and surely not Adam alone as the author of some primordial tragedy. Being free, all could sin. They were under no compulsion to do so. It was their free choice to sin, and in the train of their disobedient choice came a variety of ills.

In the Latin-speaking North African church of the late second century through the fourth century we find a similar self-confidence in human powers, but now as they had been restored through God's deed in Christ. The creature man was the conqueror, not the conquered. Eternal life was God's gift to all through baptism. Some would achieve its fullness sooner than others, either through the palm of a martyr's death or the white martyrdom of an anchorite's life. In any case, there was no necessity for the Christian to sin and there was every incentive to overcome sin totally.

We may call this spirit naive and say that it had to yield inevitably to Augustinian realism about the all-pervasiveness of sin. On the other hand we may observe that the behavior of the baptized in a tight-knit community of love ought to have been such as Cyprian, the great Carthaginian bishop, claimed. Dodds has spoken of the human warmth within the Christian community thus: "Someone was interested in them, both here and hereafter."[24] In any case, in this view no one needed to fail after the marvel of baptism.

Optimistic Views of Human Nature

In the middle of the fourth century it was common teaching that human nature tends to the good, to its own perfection. Faced with the possibility, through baptism, of a quantum leap in its grace-filled powers, it may choose that sacrament and all that follows from it. It may also sinfully reject it, or having opted for it, willfully fall away from that high calling.

E. W. Watson summarizes this outlook as follows: "If our share be so great in the work, the thought of human merit cannot be excluded; man cannot be helpless under the load of sin, nor can that load be so crushing as St. Augustine was to find it."[25] This mood should prepare us for the teaching of Pelagius (d. after 418) and his more systematic followers Celestius and Julian. They present, not a clear departure from an understood orthodoxy, but an expression of the prevailing sentiment. Creation was a grace, as were the human powers that fell within it. To be free to choose was to act on the initial gift in which God's grace almost entirely consists, the "faculty and capacity of nature."[26] Already in Pelagius' time, however, the Adam story in Genesis was being read as the divinely authored explanation of sin and death. Pelagius offended not so much in his strong vote of confidence in what humanity could do as in his assumption that sin was not to be explained by Adam's fall, transmitted through the propagation of the race by marriage and sex.[27] He saw sin, rather, as carried on by imitation. The will was as free before the first sin as after.

In view of Augustine's strenuous efforts to press for a darkened intellect and a weakened will, the times could not endure this contravention. Augustine summarized for condemnation six of Celestius' propositions which contained material that had an honorable history and was still being taught in the East. Among them were the statements that Adam was fated to die whether he sinned or not; that his sin damaged only him and not the whole human race; that newborn infants were in the same state that Adam was before his sin; and that the whole race does not die through the death and transgression of Adam.[28]

IRENAEUS ANSWERS THE HERETICS

Irenaeus, the Greek-speaking bishop of Lyons, in framing a response to the gnostic heretics produced an ordered exposition of orthodox belief such as did not exist. In his five books on *The Unmasking and Refutation of False Gnosis,* commonly designated *Against Heresies* (written 175–185), he identifies the fall of man with the sin of Adam.[29] He renders explicit in many places the Pauline teaching, often hazy in the apologists, that sin came into the world through Adam's transgression and that there is some causal connection (hinted at by Paul but not spelled out) between this event and subsequent human generations. Irenaeus also teaches that baptism does away with this taint or inheritance.[30] The first human beings, created according to the image and likeness of God, lost their likeness to him through sin. This, Christ restored.

According to Irenaeus, Paul assumed of Adam only that he disobeyed freely and that physical death resulted from his choice. There are no further mythical elements in his account. He stands solidly behind the tradition of Tatian[31] and Theophilus[32] that there is no such thing as a state of "original justice" in which man is endowed with every conceivable gift. For them, humanity is, rather, imperfect and undeveloped, literally in its infancy. Irenaeus wrote, in this vein:

> In the measure that created things are younger than the Unoriginated, they are childish and in the same measure inept and unschooled for perfect training. As with a mother nourishing her baby overrichly, . . . so God could easily have bestowed perfection on humanity from the beginning, but humanity was incapable of it, being an infant. . . . The weakness and defect were not with God but with newly formed humanity because it was not uncreated.[33]

The bishop of Lyons has little vision of a primitive pair endowed with moral and physical perfection (except when he speaks of immortality before the fall, *Presentation* 15). He sees instead a humanity capable of a deathless and incorruptible state which it will achieve gradually over long centuries. It is the outpouring of the Spirit that will effect likeness to God.[34] That likeness will be accomplished slowly from the seed implanted in our first parents at the creation. Man was innocent at the beginning but not virtuous or else he could not have sinned.[35] Irenaeus even describes him before his disobedient choice as "not yet become man." "How then expect one so recently *effectus* to be *perfectus?*"[36]

This early Greek tradition has been described as overly optimistic regarding human powers. It has also been placed in a highly favorable relation to the later Augustinian view that came to prevail in the West. Little more should be claimed for it than that it understood the Adam-Christ mythology of Paul comfortably, with a probable tipping of the scales in the direction of the meaning "in Adam's loins" when

Irenaeus uses the phrase "in Adam." Greek Christian thought viewed persons of every human epoch as free. It reposed great confidence in Christ and the saving power of baptism. A personal devil was evil but Adam merely weak and immature. The race was sinful—a fact of ordinary observation—and had been sinful ever since Adam's sin. That sin saw to it that we did not possess an endowment we might have had, immortality. It also deferred the possibility of the fullness of the divine image and likeness, which came not by slow progress but by sudden gift in the person of Jesus Christ. He possessed both endowments and held out the promise of both to all humanity.

The special virtue of the Greek understanding of the origins of human sinfulness—a condition it took to be universal —was that it did not impute the effects of a far-off transgression to later generations as individual guilt. It supposed that a myth described an actual occurrence, but it did not historicize its details in such a way as to destroy its force. It retained human freedom as the possession of every age, at the same time protecting divine power and the universality of the order of grace.

AUGUSTINE ON GRACE

Augustine was the Western father who came to be identified peculiarly with the theology of grace. It is sometimes said that he brought the church back to the NT message of salvation when it was in danger of substituting for it a doctrine of human self-improvement. There was never, in fact, any such danger. What came to the fore was an effort to keep alive the notion that creation itself, including the creation of human powers, was a great grace. Augustine never denied this but took it as a direct challenge to another truth, which it was not—the sovereignty of a gracious God in human affairs. He had as part of his data his personal need, in his struggle for chastity, and the evident condition of society.

Augustine was likewise a philosopher of the nature of God and a pioneer in the psychology of human states. Impelled by such motives, he saw an overall solution as necessary. The one he chose did not set aside human freedom but so set it in a context of divine influence that a sharp eye was needed to see how the one was sustained in the light of the other. Some of Augustine's later disciples missed the distinction altogether.

In Augustine's writings the word "grace" generally comprises the whole idea of the saving work of God. His doctrine of God was not unlike that of the pagan philosopher Plotinus (205–270). It is developed in the *Confessions*, where God is said to be the highest Being, the absolutely simple and unchangeable, whose Being is one with his qualities.[37] Joined to this philosophical conception is Augustine's biblical conviction that God is a personal will who is loving, merciful, and gracious in humanity's regard. This God is constantly at work bringing creation to perfection, communicating himself and his goodness to the world he has made. Man was meant for union with the personal God, an eternal life through the beatific vision of him, on condition of his ruling over the lower creation and obeying God in everything.[38] This plan of harmony and peace did not succeed. Man turned his back on God and interested himself only in baser matters.

Sin consists, therefore, in the misdirection of will. At the root of all sin is pride or self-sufficiency, which brings with it the illusion of total freedom. Man turns to finite creatures in the expectation that they will satisfy him. This resort to the changeable rather than the Changeless is, however, deceptive. It results in the delusion that man can accomplish good of himself without God.[39] This means that the best of human actions are tarnished with pride. The will is in thrall to evil to such an extent that it cannot do good even though it might wish to. Indeed, the desire to do good is no longer present.[40]

Because of the widespread character of wrongdoing, a larger explanation of it seems called for than perverse personal choice by the sum total of individuals. Augustine finds it in the doctrine of original sin.[41] As he develops the idea, it means that Adam—presumably a historical person—is, at his creation, in complete harmony with nature. There is no strain or tension between higher ideals and lower inclinations. God helped him with his assisting grace, with which Adam freely cooperated. In his freedom the first man could have obeyed or sinned, could have progressed from the state of *being able not to* sin or die or forsake God, to that of *being unable to* do these things. Deceived by Satan he fell, going from a condition of grace to one of sin. In his new state he forfeited assisting grace as well. The necessity of dying came with the disharmony of human powers, as the concomitant of sin and its punishment. The stage that came after the fall was Adam's *inability not to* sin or die. All humanity after Adam was under like necessity. All were "in him" when he sinned (according to Rom 5:12 in Augustine's Latin Bible).

The means of the transmission of this bad inheritance is the body, for whoever is conceived in concupiscence must be ruled by it. To original sin is added the guilt of personal sins, making each individual a mass of evildoing and liable to eternal loss. Even the best thoughts and deeds are contaminated by the tragedy of self-love. In our sinful condition, we can barely recognize the good. We long for it restlessly. "Humanity, using free will badly, lost both free will and itself."[42] Augustine seems to hold that the only freedom remaining is to do ill, not good. The search for happiness continues but is carried out in the wrong place.[43] To Augustine's credit, it must be said that he is not an individualist in his view of human life but that he sees the consequences of sin in interlocking lives and generations.

As outlined, this doctrine was not readily defensible as part of the familiar Catholic tradition which had held out so long against gnostic dualism. The saving features were the insistence that human nature is not in itself evil but only worsened, and that salvation continues to be available to weakened humanity from outside itself by the grace of God. At this point Augustine's thought joins up with Paul's, Paul who has no doctrine of Adamic harmony or hereditary transmission of guilt or diminished human powers. Augustine puts grace in the realm of divinity, where it belongs. He does not see humanity capable of lodging a claim against God that God must honor:

> Grace is not grace unless it is freely given. Even the meritorious deeds of man must therefore be understood as gifts of God.[44]

God saves a human race that would otherwise be lost by honoring his own gift of the Spirit which he sees there. We are reconciled by Christ the mediator and accept through him the Holy Spirit, who changes us from enemies of God to friends. It is by grace alone, the grace of God through Jesus Christ, that we are liberated from evil. Without it we achieve absolutely nothing good in thought, will, love, or action.[45] In support of this position—or better, in illustration of it—Augustine cites 2 Cor 13:7. There Paul petitions for the community at Corinth the "inspiration of good will and deed," that they may leave off doing works of evil.

It should be evident why this fairly simple solution to the problem of sin recommended itself to the bishop of Hippo. It preserves all that needs to be preserved, or so he is convinced, and accounts for insoluble divine mystery in the same breath. Any failure by creatures to acknowledge the right order that God has created in the universe or to act on it is not only pride but idolatry—a putting of the creature in the Creator's place. The offense is so enormous that Augustine was blind to the possibility that he might have misprized the worth of human beings before God in his proposed solution. He was convinced that he knew their only true worth —namely, in God. He further thought, with Paul, that salvation was a meaningless idea if there were no human race in need of it, and if the creature in need of saving could save itself.

OBJECTIONS TO AUGUSTINE

Augustine's opponents did not hold his doctrine of God against him. Rather, it was his assumption, which he thought he found in Scripture and in life, that the race was fallen, in the sense that its will was turned against God. They also had trouble with his theory of the body as the transmitter of a disobedient nature once Adam's sin had been committed. Those who accepted his teaching on original sin, its mode of transmission quite apart, still had the problem that he seemed to glorify grace by belittling nature and free will. Faustus of Riez (d. ca. 490) pointed out that, in the sources, the grace of God was featured at one time and the will of man at another, in an unresolved tension. He held that settling the question in terms of human freedom was a mistake but so was resolving it exclusively in terms of grace.[46] John Cassian (d. 435) thought it went against the "rule of faith" to attempt an answer to an insoluble mystery.[47] Augustine's chief departure from the tradition of the fathers was held to be his teaching that God called only the elect in accord with his decree. He knew as well as anyone the text of 1 Tm 2:4 which taught the universal call to salvation, but he interpreted "all" to be all the predestined, among whom every kind of human being was represented.[48] For him the passage said that no one is saved unless God wills it.[49]

Augustine's opponents summed up his teaching by saying that "God does not desire all men to be saved but only the fixed number of the predestined,"[50] and they were not wrong. The chief charge they leveled against him was that of fatalism,[51] saying that under the appearance of Christian doctrine he was teaching the necessity of sin and death for some. And, indeed, his system was highly vulnerable for its lack of distinction between the divine foreknowledge and efficient grace. Augustine's principle was that the will of God must always achieve its intended purpose. To be logical, he might have read the text that says God "desires all men to be saved and come to a knowledge of the truth" as a declaration of universal salvation. He was too sure of sin and damnation for that. "All men" had to mean all who were predestined to glory, not the remainder.

A final difficulty against the doctor of grace was his seeming lack of support for Paul when the latter held that the gentiles do by nature what the law requires (Rom 2: 14). Some of Augustine's backers said that only the gentiles who were later converted to Christ were meant. Others said that Roman and Greek *honestas* was all that was intended—a natural decency that fell far short of the virtue of the saved. This was Prosper of Aquitaine's response to John Cassian.[52] But the Augustinian opponents were not satisfied. They thought they knew too many good pagans, or at least enough whose wills had not been taken captive. They saw seeds of goodness planted in every soul by the Creator. Faustus of Riez wrote: "Anyone who denies that nature is to be proclaimed in its good qualities simply does not know that the Author of nature is the same as the Author of grace. . . . Since the creator is the same as the Restorer, one and the same is celebrated when we praise either work."[53] As Pelikan comments, "Praising the free will of man meant praising its Creator and did not detract from his grace."[54]

The church generally went with an anti-Pelagian view of grace, but it did not follow Augustine in his theory of predestination, much as he might have thought the two inseparable.

But as a church it had little praise to offer those who saved it from a near-miss. Their valorous stand was stigmatized as "semi-Pelagian." In the words of Prosper, they held on to the "remnants of the Pelagian perversity."[55]

SUMMARY

The first five centuries of the church's life yield the following data:

—In the early (i.e., post-apostolic) period, stress was laid on the continuity of Christian life with human life as viewed by the philosophers; less so—starting with Justin—on continuity with Jewish life, where minor ritual and cultural differences were seized upon to heighten the differences and establish Christian superiority.

—Primary among the early explanations of sin and evil was demonic power, even though others such as the "evil impulse" in humanity, the Eden narrative, and the Watchers narrative were cited frequently. Gradually the garden story predominated because of Paul's attributing human mortality to Adam's sin, with diabolic influence retained through identifying the serpent with Satan.

—The Greek fathers, preoccupied with divine changelessness and its human counterpart achieved through immortality, concentrated on death as the chief effect of the "fall," while the Latin fathers favored the transmission of sin and guilt. Both came to be convinced that these primordial events, which they took to be historical, constituted the catastrophe that required redemption.

—God was viewed as unfailingly gracious to mankind, but as stress on his proximity and love in Jesus Christ increased, an appreciation of his favor to the human race and to the Jews in particular, before the incarnation, receded. So strong did this emphasis become that the entire revelation to Israel was reduced to a type of foreshadowing, while the graciousness of providential care was, in effect, removed from the category of grace. For the Eastern fathers, baptism brought divinization, or the restoration to humanity of the likeness to God lost with Adam's sin; for the West, it removed the effects of hereditary sin, with the exception of passionate desire. Both were agreed that only in Christ was humanity as it had been in Adam and divinely meant to be without interruption: deathless, sinless, whole.

—The East maintained with some success the mythic character of sin, which was the countervailing force to grace in the Pauline reading of cosmic history. Paradoxically, Augustine's pioneering work in human drives and motives (which had no Eastern counterpart) was either blunted or used incorrectly because of his supposition that Paul generally meant by "sin" individual acts of human choice.

—The view of the cosmos as a unity and humanity as its visible spokesman led to mythic constructs of the entire creation as out of harmony with God's purpose, ever since angelic and human sin. Paul's statement about the groaning of all creation as it awaited deliverance contributed to this outlook (Rom 8: 22f.). As a result, the Christian fathers came to feature disharmony in nature more than harmony and to impugn the pagan philosophers who, in their optimism, laid stress on its balance.

—In general, patristic unfamiliarity with Hebrew thought led the church fathers to reckon biblical concentration on the present life and a lack of interest in immortality a matter of gross imperfection, and to consider the this-worldly eon thought of the NT to be concerned with an immortal life in heaven. This led to a vigorous condition of hope in God's future, of a kind proper to the Jews and to the apostolic age, but also to a relativizing and misprizing of earthly life that the NT cannot be accused of if its eschatological thought is understood. The Greek and Latin fathers did so misunderstand it by viewing it literally in the light of their preconceptions.

Chapter VII

IMPLICATIONS
FOR CONTEMPORARY FAITH

It has been correctly said that ideas have consequences. There is today a Christian world that is paradoxically respectful of ancient Israel and contemptuous of Jews, that is guilt-ridden yet withheld by few restraints, that revels in its freedom but is afraid to act freely. Let us, in this chapter, try to see why.

This study has addressed two basic questions: Was Christianity in its founding documents committed to the superiority of spirit over matter with its consequent low view of human and worldly realities? And did it teach the succession—chronological or ontological—of an order of nature by an order of grace? If so, did this put the Law of the Jews and the power of reason of non-Jews in a secondary, even reprobated position?

An exploration of most of the NT books disclosed that whereas the general drift of later Christianity was set in them, they have little to say on certain issues of great modern concern. They speak much of law and grace, but little of grace and nature. It is, in fact, almost impossible to extract from them a theory of the creation of human life as it might have existed apart from God's deed in Jesus Christ. Indeed, 1 Tm 4:4 is unique in the NT in declaring: "Everything God created is good; nothing is to be rejected when it is received with thanksgiving."

A brief inquiry into the writings of the church fathers on the subject of grace in Christ concluded the study. The im-

portant developments of the patristic period on the relation
of Christ to God and of the Holy Spirit to both were not
considered. Neither were the implications of the enforced
clerical abstention from sex prescribed by the Council of
Elvira in Spain (ca. 305), nor the unsuccessful effort in the
same line at Nicea in 325. The overall unsympathetic, not to
say hostile, record of the fathers to life under the Mosaic Law
was likewise omitted. Finally, the post-patristic theological
edifices of the East and the West—which have proved to be
more directly influential on modern thought than the works
of their giant predecessors—have been passed by.

The evangelists, Paul, and the fathers were all theologians
of the church. Because of the inspired character attributed
to the NT writings, there is no avenue so fruitful for Christian
reflection as an inquiry into the meaning of the NT books.
The settlements that are meaningful in the lives of Christians
are those arrived at by the various communions through the
teachings of bishops and synods, creeds and catechisms. Yet
all such teachings go back to the NT as they have reached us
through the theological activity of the patristic era. To know
where the church has come from is to have some idea of
where it should be going if it is to remain faithful to God in
Christ and in the Spirit. What the NT teaches about God and
world, nature and grace, and grace as made manifest in the
Abrahamic covenant, Mosaic Law, and Christ crucified and
risen is crucial. It was the right place to begin the search,
however unrewarding it may have proved in certain areas.

Perhaps the single most important fact to emerge from the
preceding chapters has been the virtual silence of the NT on
whether human life is part of the continuum of a creation
good in God's sight. The NT assumes human freedom to act
despite the "given" of human sinfulness. It does not say
whether or how it thinks humanity is good when it is not
acting disobediently toward God. The reasons for the NT's
silence are fairly clear. Inspired Scripture, for its authors, was
the Bible of the Jews in the Septuagint version. The biblical
books affirmed the goodness of creation on every page. There

was no need for the Christians to repeat it, in writings that did not set out consciously to be "Scripture" in any case. (Only 2 Pt 3:15f. intimates that Paul's difficult letters might be on a par with the earlier collection; 2 Tm 3:15f. contains a similar thought, phrased even more ambiguously.) The preachers and teachers of the NT who testified to the message about God's deed in Christ confined their efforts to two matters chiefly: his own teachings, and the implications of his resurrection for the Jews who awaited a promised salvation and the gentiles who learned of it by God's mercy. Confining themselves thus to the problem of the divine fidelity, the NT writers felt no need to reaffirm the Jewish world view. For them it was already in possession.

MAN'S UNITY WITH ALL CREATION

A few observations are in order. First of all, that world view knew of the affinity of humanity with the clay of the ground (Gn 2:7). The first creature is called "the man" throughout *(ha 'adam)*, in a word cognate with "ruddy" (earth?) or the Akkadian "made," "formed." His wife is called *Havvah*, a word that bears a resemblance to "life," because she is the mother of all the living (Gn 3:20). Despite its earthy origins, the pair is not featured as continuous with other creatures but as having dominion over all the rest (Gn 1:28). In a separate account, the man is the namer of all the birds and beasts, among whom he finds no suitable partner (Gn 2:20). The two creation accounts were combined after the exile; one of them, the narrative of the six days, was written after the exile. Placed at the head of the collection of books, however, they set the tone for all that followed.

Humanity is a part of the very earth, yet it stands above and apart from all in being created, as God says, "in our image, after our likeness" (Gn 1:26). The likeness of humanity to creatures that are even less like God than man and woman is seldom subsequently mentioned. The Bible stressed the distinctiveness of humanity. This was a splendid contribution, since the ancient world was alive with a pessimism that emphasized life's futility. It knew man as no better than the beasts. Despite this ancient advantage of the Bible, the information amassed over the last few centuries on the unity of life on the planet earth—a unity known to various other peoples through religious insight—has caused the Bible's silences to be damaging to Jew and Christian alike. God has other tongues than the scriptural, but the Christian community, for one, has been loath to use them. Christianity as a credible faith tradition has been the loser through the testimonies to God it has not acknowledged.

One thinks, for example, of the ways in which Asian, American Indian, and African religions, especially those committed to the one God, are at ease in speaking and praying about the unity of all things. In these thought worlds the human race has a common lot with all creatures. The absence of this theme from the NT has been most influential. Even in such well-known psalms as Pss 148 and 150, and in the magnificent song of the three men delivered from the fiery furnace (which occurs in the deuterocanonical material that follows Dn 3:23) where identity with creation is mentioned, the stress is more on the greatness of the Creator and the way his creatures praise him than on the lot that creatures have in common.

The creeds of Christianity are for the most part voiceless on the basic truth of the unity of all creation. In the midst of the gnostic attack at full force, the sum total of the church's pronouncements was that the one God was Father and the "maker of heaven and earth" or of "all things, seen and unseen." It was important for the church, in a world of demiurge and pleroma, to proclaim boldly that there was no god but the one God; that no being, angelic or demonic, existed apart from his creative word. Yet the church was strangely mute on the great cosmological questions that were rending it. Whether this was out of fear that its legions of angels and hosts of demons might bring it close to the excesses of the

Gnostics, or out of hesitancy to implicate the cosmos too heavily in the religious venture as the Gnostics had done, is hard to say. Whatever the case, the church forwent official statements, from earliest times until now, on the nature of the world that God has made and humanity as part of it. By and large, it let the Bible speak for it. Speculative intellects like Origen (d. ca. 254) and Clement of Alexandria (d. before 215), Augustine (d. 430), Leibniz (d. 1716), and Teilhard de Chardin (d. 1955) have come to grips with some of these problems. In every case the church has dealt with its thinkers ambivalently: in suspicion as they anticipated questions not yet officially dealt with; in a mixture of repudiation in their own time and grudging gratitude centuries later. The ambivalence is thoroughgoing in that these speculations are pointed to with pride when the test of time sustains them, but when time proves them false, as if the church had never had a part in them.

Simplistic responses to major dilemmas from Christians who are convinced that the Bible resolves every doubt is a familiar phenomenon. The churches that entertain the full range of modern problems on sophisticated terms, however, are often remarkably silent when it comes to affirming certain basic truths about human life. When they do so, they are content with generalities from the Bible or from the fathers which are true enough in their mythic framework but inadequate to the modern challenge.

The unwillingness to put the full weight of church authority behind what may prove to be ephemeral opinion is understandable. There are also the churches for whom there is no authority but that of the Bible. Hence the Bible's silences are the churches' silences. But when all is said and done, the larger communions that have shown no hesitation in preaching NT salvation in Jesus Christ seem to have shirked an important obligation. They have not preached about human and subhuman life on the earth in such a way as to remove the barriers that exist for many to the acceptance of salvation.

Papal utterances to learned groups or position papers at
global assemblies of the World Council of Churches are not
the kind of teaching that is formative. The effective media in
the churches are the creeds and liturgies, sermons and
hymns that have the force of repetition in the lives of mil-
lions. The spareness and strength of creedal language, in
which the limited but constantly reiterated phrases convey
conviction about basic truth, are needed, but lacking.

IS THE CREATED ORDER GOOD?

The great formularies of faith and prayer in the Christian
church are seriously deficient in the manner in which they
speak—or do not speak—of the importance of the world to
God down to the least creature. They tend not to affirm
creation's basic homogeneity and goodness, having early
been deflected by theories of salvation that felt constrained
to speak ill of it in its present state. The effects of this omis-
sion, or affirmation of defect, are devastating to the Christian mentality. When Christians say, "God loves the world,
but . . ." or "God loves sinful humanity, but . . ," the negative statement that follows the conjunction tends to out-
weigh the positive one that precedes it. The effect in practice is one that no Christian or Christian church can
tolerate in theory: a determination of God by creatures; a
world in which the bad appears to govern the good.

The IV Council of the Lateran (1215) defined against the
Albigenses and the Cathari that the one true God, Father,
Son, and Spirit, was the one principle of all things, the creator
of the seen and unseen both spiritual and corporal. It goes on:

> By his almighty power he constituted simultaneously from the
> beginning of time the spiritual and the bodily, the angelic and
> the this-worldly creation from nothing; then the human, con-
> stituted, so to say, by spirit and body in common. The devil
> and other demons were by nature created good by God but

became evil by their own doing. Humanity sinned at the instance of the devil.

The definition continues to say that the Holy Trinity first gave saving teaching through Moses, the prophets, and other servants of God. Finally, God's only son Jesus Christ, having become man, showed the way of life more clearly. The language from that point on is familiarly creedal on the manner in which salvation operates, including Christ's mortality and capacity to suffer as human and his coming to judge the living and the dead: "He will render to each according to his (her) works, both the reprobate and the elect." All will rise with their own bodies, the ones they now have, to receive just recompense for their deeds, "some to perpetual punishment with the devil, others to eternal glory with Christ."[1] The pro-matter thrust of this declaration is evident. So is the seriousness with which it takes fallen angelic creatures, as if they had an essential part in the drama of human salvation. It would be repeated at Florence (1442) and I Vatican (1870).

Even this IV Lateran statement was not nearly so specific as a profession of faith prescribed for the Waldensians of Tarragona (1208) that goes back to the time of Peter Waldo (1179–1181). There, God is called the creator, maker, governor, and disposer of all things corporal and spiritual, visible and invisible, heavenly and also on the land, in the sea, and in the air. Some teaching on the church, priestly power, and sacraments follows, concluding with the statement that fleshly marriages are to be entered into. For the latter, 1 Cor 7 is cited. There are affirmations that man and wife are to be saved together and that second and further marriages are not to be condemned. The eating of meat is held to be not blameworthy. Capital punishment by the state is permissible when it is decided upon prudently and not out of revenge or hatred (an addition of 1210). The devil is as he is, not by nature, but by his evil will. We shall rise in the body we go about in. The good works proposed by James (2:17) are essential. We should therefore renounce what we have and give to the poor, using no more money or clothing than daily need requires, since the evangelical counsels (presumably of poverty, chastity, and obedience) are to be kept as commandments.[2]

Normally, Christian creeds and councils abstain from ethical statements about the ordinary conduct of life. That is why the teaching of IV Lateran, despite its limitations, stands out like a beacon. Salvation in Christ is total, taking effect on all of life from the moment of baptism. Yet it is usually presented as something only fully realized in an age to come. A healthy anticipation of the glorious life after death tends to blunt the sensitivity to the importance of the present life, and even to obscure the glory of being baptized.

WICKEDNESS IN HIGH PLACES

In the NT, the "unclean spirits," "powers in high places," and "the devil and his angels" are assumed to have a free, creaturely existence in complete subordination to the all-holy God. Strictly speaking, they threaten his dominion not at all. While they are his enemies by their own choice, it is not he who is their peer but the angels of light. Less than their peers by nature are their human fellow creatures. In no sense did Christian faith, any more than Judaism, pit Satan against God in an equal contest.

Despite this fact, the notion of angels and devils so seized the popular imagination that both—but the devils in particular—became a featured part of Christian teaching. Diabolic influence rather than an attraction to evil freely yielded to become the explanation of most that was awry in life. The apologists and church fathers had two strong sources in this matter: the words attributed by the evangelists to Jesus and the gnostic-tinged vocabulary of the Pauline writings, and the readiness of the Jewish and pagan worlds to accept the reality of unseen intelligences inimical to the human race. As a result, not only was demonic activity never repudiated by

Christianity, it was let free to flourish as an essential factor in human life.

The trend began as early as the apostolic preaching (e.g., Ac 10:38). In two hundred years, the tempting by Satan as the serpent was identified as the cause of the first human sin and the root cause of the need of redemption. The devil had not been an essential figure in Jesus' teaching. Neither was he such in the presentation of the evangelists, of Paul, or the other NT writers. For all of them he remained what he was in post-biblical Judaism, a shadowy symbol of evil. In second- and third-century Christianity, however, he became a clear personage in the history of the human race, where he has remained ever since.

The devil and the demons of hell thus came to have an importance in Christian life out of all proportion to their place in the NT. This arose chiefly through reading the details of the garden story literally as essential to the Christ-Adam myth. In the gospels, whoever or whatever the "unclean spirits" are, they are treated by Jesus with perfect mastery and contempt. Not only did the demons progress from NT ambiguity to clarity in Christian history, they became a countervailing force to God. While technically retaining creaturely status, their power for evil not only far surpassed the power of the angels for good but even approached the divine. The Christian faith has been saddled with this studied ambivalence regarding devils ever since.

In the church's official teaching there is no opposite principle to God. In practices like exorcism, which flourished in all the baptismal liturgies of East and West (not to speak of much later aberrations such as the hunt for witches), the devils come so close to being an opposite principle of evil that Christians are hard put to tell the difference. Only when the prince of this realm is divinized does the church say "heresy." Short of that, he is allowed to flourish as a myth so lively that the fullness of divine power and holiness are imperiled.

In every age, including the present one, the power of demons is reiterated. This is usually done under two rationales: one, that the NT requires acceptance of this power, and therefore those who deny diabolic influence deny the Scriptures; and, two, that the enormity of evil is such that no mere human explanation can account for it. The difficulty with this position for Christian orthodoxy is twofold. First, a minor them in NT soteriology becomes a major one. Neither Jesus, Paul, nor any NT writer views the devil and his legions as the root of all human evil. Secondly and far worse, the supremacy of God as creator is threatened, while his power as redeemer and sanctifier through the Son and the Spirit is likewise called into question.

The only dualism that NT Christianity admits is an ethical one—the opposition of disobedient creatures to God. While the major concern of the post-apostolic church with diabolical activity preserves the letter of this sole dualism, the door is opened in spirit to another, a metaphysical dualism that cannot be allowed. This requires that the immeasurable boon of salvation in Christ be taught forcefully by the church without recourse to a satanic influence on human sinfulness which is largely absent from the NT sources. Whatever the usefulness of the development from the second through the fifth century—and with hindsight even this may be questioned—it clearly is not helpful in understanding God's sovereign goodness and human responsibility before him. Accepting the holiness of an unseen God is a sufficient challenge to faith without making the activity of a myriad unseen principle of evil a condition of it. Attractive though this belief has always been, its net effect is to incline Christians to a dualist universe, to diminish their trust in the power of God, and to reduce their attention to the possibilities for evil lurking in the human heart.

CURBING HARMFUL CONCEPTS

Mythic constructs that prove more harmful than helpful to belief in salvation by a holy God must therefore be curbed. If he is to be served, the imaginative promotion of evil creatures to quasi-divine status must be curbed. Christian preaching should not by any means set aside the NT proposition that Christ overcame the power of evil, including the demonic. But this real and generic conquest has little to do with the myth of a diabolic tempter who first enticed the human race to sin and who continues to be influential as a spirit whose hold is yet unbroken.

This demand that the church be faithful to its best teaching is necessarily accompanied by a call to repudiate positively a mythic "fall." This is not a revival of the hoary demand for a "religion of reason." It is, rather, a demand lodged by the Bible itself. There, it is clearly said that humanity has been prone to disobedience to God from its beginnings. No biblical · teaching that purports to be true as human history holds that things were ever any different from now. Certain church fathers like Athanasius taught freely that death is the condition of creaturely life—unavoidable, given the complex and mutable kind of creature a human being is (cf. *On the Incarnation* 5). When Genesis proposes the origins of man and woman, of sin and death, of drudgery, childbearing, and the attraction and repulsion of the sexes, it is palpably operating in the mythic genre. To single out one of these etiological legends for literal understanding, while correctly interpreting the others, is a grave offense against the nature of the Bible.

There is a biblical vision of humanity in harmony and integrity apart from sin, to be sure. But it is a vision. It is not the record of a time when the conditions of life and death were different from those of subsequent ages. That the human race is in a state of decline from what it might have been or might be, there is no doubt. That humanity is sinful and has been so from its origins is a conclusion demanded by all that we know of history, even if there were not a powerful biblical tale to underscore it. But because there is such a tale which for Christians comprises divinely inspired teaching, they have a serious obligation to avoid literalizing it lest they destroy its meaning.

The Christian church possesses a doctrine of original sin in its uninterrupted teaching that Jesus Christ saves from the twin condition in which humanity finds itself from its beginnings. That condition is one of disobedience to God or sin, and mortality. The two are inextricably linked in that both go back to human origins, but not by any historical cause-effect relation that is demonstrably a biblical revelation. The Genesis story holds for such a relation, it is true. Paul confirms it. Neither author, however, offends against the mythic genre. Yet this is precisely what the non-Jewish church fathers began to do almost immediately by taking cause and effect to be a matter of actual history, not of myth. Like the rabbis, they speculated on the condition of Adam and Eve before they sinned. Unlike them, they assumed a historical time during which all things human were as God would have had them apart from sin. For almost two millennia Christian faith was transmitted, not strained, by this imaginative interpretation. For the past two centuries the bedrock truth of salvation from sin has been more imperiled than aided by the literal presentation of the tale, or the semi-literal retention of certain of its features.

God's saving work must, by definition, be credible, i.e., a possible object of faith. Through wrong interpretations like the one outlined above, it becomes incredible. This is needless. No biblical teaching is at stake, only the early (not primitive) misapprehension of biblical teaching. This is compounded in some circles by a new literalism, the illegitimate offspring of the principle that the terms of salvation are to be found "in Scripture alone."

Augustine was not the sole offender in regard to Eden and

the origins of human evil. This is a fact despite the strong impression made on the West by his version of the doctrine of original sin. In another form, beginning with Origen, the doctrine already had acceptance in the East. In the modern period, neither West nor East is culturally open to it as it was formulated after A.D. 150, be it a question of hereditary descent from Adam or imitation of his example. *Clearly there must be a return to the teaching in its NT form, which is the symbolism of two distinct epochs.*

There must also be an unequivocal indication by the church in modern times that Paul's Adam-Christ figure is but one way of conveying the truth that in Christ God's grace overcomes sin. A literal interpretation of Gn 3 has no part in the symbolic use of Adam, whose appearance as the first human being is identical with his role as first sinner. The true mythic nature of Paul's eon theology must be recovered if it is to be of any use. Paul's development in Romans is a myth of another sort than that of the garden, but no less a myth. Its purpose as he conceived it was to teach the divine goodness as the complete vanquisher of human evil. He did *not* mean to instruct literally about a human history before Christ when all went ill, followed by a time since then when all goes well. Christianity has an unspecified eschatological hope. It has no matching protohistory of paradisal beginnings.

The creeds of the first three centuries are our safe guide. By extracting the NT data that were thought essential for a person to profess for baptism, they featured the saving deeds of God and omitted any theory of the origins of sin. Those deeds were: God's creative activity; the death, resurrection, and glorification of Jesus Christ and his sure return as judge; and the works of the Spirit such as the church, the forgiveness of sins taken globally, the resurrection of the body, and the life of the age to come. This mixture of history and myths which interpret history avoids historicizing the biblical accounts of the origins of sin.

Two Modes of Salvation

The Pauline way of understanding the mystery of God's gracious love is not the only one proposed by the NT. It is probably not the way best suited to our times because of our weak sense of the power of myth. The evangelists presented the truth of salvation in various ways, but basically in two. Of these, belief in the saving power of Jesus' teaching is the clearer. Jesus exercises this power in conjunction with his death and resurrection in a way they do not spell out. Paul, for his part, featured faith in Christ's death and resurrection as saving, and reduced the teaching of Jesus as saving, to a few paraphrased "sayings of the Lord." Paraenetic teaching in NT books other than the gospels and Paul continues the tradition begun with the preaching of Jesus. There are calls to repentance, to obedience to God's commands, to fulfilling his will through deeds of justice and mercy. This NT approach to salvation in Christ assumes the effectiveness of his obedience unto death. This death was responded to by God, who raised him in glory. That there must be faith—trust in God acting through Christ—the evangelists, 1 and 2 Peter, James, and the others never doubt. They do not, however, isolate faith as the sole means of receiving the benefits of salvation. And they mean by faith, not all that Paul means, but the simpler, biblical reliance on God as the savior of his people. They couple this trust in his saving goodness with the necessity of doing his will.

Thus, 1 Peter (an epistle that reflects Pauline thought) speaks of deliverance by Christ's blood beyond price which makes people become believers in the God who raised him from the dead (1 Pt 1:18–21). Yet this writer likewise exhorts to intense ethical activity, including arming oneself with the outlook that was Christ's (4:1).

There is, in a word, a complete confidence in human capacity in the many hortatory passages of the NT books. Of human nature maimed, weakened, or darkened there is no record. This notion can be arrived at only by extrapolating uncritically from references to passion and desire, which hint at some primordial catastrophe as their cause. The church fathers whose training had been influenced by the Greek philosophers began with the conviction that humanity in its perfect form was passionless. This had to be the condition, therefore, of the first pair as they came from the Creator's hand. At the point of the primordial sin reason lost its control over the bodily appetites, leading to the innate condition of concupiscence. That such aggressiveness or ardor of the passions might have been a perfection of the human species, not its imperfection, and not identical at all points with the inclination to evil, was beyond the grasp of these devotees of apathy.

In the NT, humanity is free. It can and must choose. God will reward or punish according to the choice that is made. Even Paul—to whom another view has been falsely attributed—is quite clear on this, in passages like Rom 2:6ff.; 1 Cor 3:8; 2 Cor 5:10. In human nature there is an inclination to do wrong, but there is also a strong inclination to do right. No primordial occurrence is required to explain the lack of perfect balance. The complexity of the body-spirit creature that is humanity, coupled with the sins of the entire race, explain it sufficiently. Particularly influential are those long-standing sins of tribe, nation, and family which are the burden of each newborn child. This statement makes no genetic claim, only a cultural and historical one. Original sin is a reality because no one is born free of the influence of the sins committed by all from the beginning.

The fact of sin is a consequence of the Creator's decision to make angelic and human creatures free. He could have made goodness the only attractive option by creating free beings in his presence—the assumption of the life of heaven. But having placed humanity on the earth, the home of this race, he allowed not only the possibility but the likelihood of choice against him. The necessity of sin did not exist. Human-

ity was always free and never without the divine assistance.
The Bible features the fact of sin without speculating about
a time in history that was without it. It does precisely the
opposite. In its various affirmations of the universality of
human sinfulness (one of which, the Eden account comple-
mented by the figure of the two races in Adam and in Christ,
emerged as central), the Bible states that God's goodness is
greater than humanity's resistance to his goodness. It will
prevail.

The Christian Scriptures concentrate on a special aspect of
the God-world relationship, the salvation of all that is human
through his son Jesus Christ. They do not contain a fundamental teaching on the alienation of all creation from God or
the essential lostness of the human race. Some Christian
teachers, to be sure, have taken their cue from some phrases
of Paul or the Johannine writings and taught the one or the
other. The church—more through its silences or unthought-
out repetition of Pauline formulas than positive presentation
—has let the supposition flourish that either or both were its
teaching. But there is no doctrine of the whole church that
God was ever at odds with the cosmos, that humanity was
given over to evil, or that God saves it apart from the free
exercise of human choice.

Phrases such as the traditional ones that "Christ takes our
guilt upon himself" or "saves the world from sin and death"
are true for Christians, but they must be proclaimed in such
a way that no impression is given of humanity as an actor in
a divinely directed puppet show. Christ does not achieve
salvation for a race that must abdicate its own responsibility
as the price. Whatever theory of salvation is adopted—and
the NT suggests several—the fact remains that sin is nearly
universal in the human heart. Universal redemption in
Christ is a means to the free obedience and service that God
has always sought from his creatures. Neither "fallenness" in
sin nor "upraising" in grace—metaphors from bodily posture
—has any magic or automatic quality. The relationships of
human beings to God and to each other are always poten-

tially personal, even though culture and environment may have reduced this element to near the zero point. At no time, whether in a human condition of sin or grace, does God deal with his creatures apart from their freedom. Not everything they do is a human act, but when they act humanly they act freely. This will be the case whether the choice is in accord with his saving grace or resists it.

LAW AND GRACE

This "saving" reality of grace is primarily God himself. He is traditionally designated, with perfect appropriateness, "uncreated Grace." Salvation is the difference accomplished by God in the creature who approaches full humanity by allowing proximity to the divine. In biblical times salvation was literally a saving from death at the hands of enemies. Redemption likewise was the purchase of a people enslaved, whether literally (as in Egypt or Babylon) or figuratively (as from their sins and offenses). As the Jews came on to the bitter periods first of Greek, then Roman domination, the dream of political freedom as a means to total freedom never died. Some began to look for a freedom that was certain in an age to come. They saw in the knowledge of God and obedience to his commands their means of release from all the captivities of the present age.

So much was this the mood of Judaism in Jesus' day that he could have preached no message to his people that they would have understood except one of deliverance through obedience to the Law. Such is the record of his preaching. We know from the symbolic interpretations of the Law found in Philo of Alexandria and the writings of the Dead Sea communities some of the latitude that was abroad on what it meant to fulfill the Law. The emerging rabbinic settlement was by no means monolithic. That the Christian understanding came closer to Philo and Qumrân should cause no great surprise. Yet Jesus' teaching on conformity to God's will that

lay behind the commands was also the teaching of Johanan
ben Zakkai, Judah the Patriarch, and others on the observance of these commandments. Jesus did not oppose specific
precepts so much as stress intent. His attention to popular
abuses in the promulgation of the oral Law seems to be what
tipped the scales in the direction of his seeming anti-Law
mentality.

The resistance of Paul to the rabbinic interpretation of
Law fulfillment resulted from his conviction that it led to
Law justification but not faith justification. Paul's teaching
made the cleavage between the rabbis and the diaspora followers of Jesus complete. There was no necessity that things
should have worked out as they did. All Jewish parties, not
just the Christian, held for conformity to the spirit of the Law
and not its letter. Paul's peculiar interpretation of Jewish eon
thought—namely, that the entire first eon was under sin and
the second eon under grace—made the difference.

Viewing Christ as the fulfillment of every biblical type,
Paul saw in the Mosaic dispensation an interim device in the
life of the people that had begun with the covenant of faith
struck with Abraham. Paul did not have to view the Law as
he did. Nothing in the teaching of Jesus required it. But it
proved to be a practical expedient, helping him to gain admission for gentiles into the believing community on equal
terms. He reports in Gal 2:10 that the only stipulation the
Jerusalem church made was that he should be mindful of the
poor, while Ac 15 tells of the far better known settlement
that probably derived from Lucan theology. The destructive
effects of Paul's theory on Jewish believers in Christ could not
have been foreseen by him. No doubt he thought that by
attributing a corrosive character to Law observance all he
had done was point out to Jews and gentiles alike the danger
to both of laying claims upon God.[3]

Other witnesses to the apostolic preaching took a different
route. Like Paul, they saw fulfillment of the Law in discipleship of Christ. Unlike him, they engaged in little formal argument to set anyone free from its precepts. Important excep-

tions are Ac 10:9–23 (Peter's vision of clean and unclean foods) and occasional sayings attributed to Jesus such as Mk 7:19*b* and 10:11–12. They promulgated instead certain positive interpretations that summed up the whole Law, such as love of God and fellow countryman (Mark), the higher righteousness (Matthew), or the kingly law of freedom (James). In these radical principles of interpretation, the NT writers resembled the Righteous Teacher of Qumrân if not the allegorical approach of Philo. None of them, including Paul, distinguished between the ethical requirements of the Law that had to be kept and the dietary and cultic perscriptions that did not.

In summary, all the Christians of the apostolic age assumed that the whole Law had to be observed. The non-Pauline churches did so by reinterpreting what was meant by the Law (the technique of the rabbis), Paul and his churches by declaring Christ the end toward which the Law pointed. For Paul, its letter no longer bound on condition of faith in Christ.

Two different seeds were thus planted by two sets of apostolic preachers, with still a third represented by the Jewish Christians of Jerusalem. Whether the latter in fact granted the concessions attributed to James in Ac 15:13–21 or proposed some other terms we do not know. The gradual gentilizing of the church achieved by Paul's preaching and the events of A.D. 66–70 led to a bifurcation in the way the Jewish Scriptures were read in the church. One path taken was that of Justin, Pseudo-Barnabas, and others. They retained the biblical writings while directly opposing what their Jewish contemporaries made of them. The other was that of The Didache, 1 Clement, and Hermas, who continued to stress fidelity to the commandments but on an interpretative principle different from that of the rabbis. The widespread acceptance of the Pauline writings as Scripture brought the latter benign interpretation of the Law to an end. The gentile church came to think it had in Paul's epistles a charter to abrogate the Law, even while it was canonizing other writings that commanded its fulfillment. The practical settlement that emerged, while not fully consistent with the Jewish Christian writings, was: "Ethical demands, yes; ritual demands, no."

By the year 200 the anti-Jewish sentiments of a gentile church were so firmly fixed that the question went further unexamined. The modified Noachian precepts of Ac 15 that bound gentile Christians, if indeed they ever did, disappeared without a trace. Baptism succeeded circumcision as the initiatory rite for all, even Jews. A fasting discipline that was professedly different from that of the Jews was adopted (cf. Didache 8:1). The law that had to be kept was that of charity and upright behavior, with no cultic, dietary, or hygienic precepts remaining.

Gradually a set of liturgical and disciplinary practices entered into church life that differed from those of Jews but were based solidly on those found in Mosaic Law. Thus, a Christian priesthood developed to which was assigned a leadership function in the ritual meal that came to be viewed as a cultic act of sacrifice. The notion of ritual purity was introduced through a celibate monastic class, a celibate episcopate, and in the West a celibate lower clergy. The Christian Pasch and Pentecost, each with its ensuing season, originated in the East on a Jewish model (the Nativity alone having sprung from a Greco-Roman model in the West). Penance and almsgiving began to flourish in the church along with fasting, as they continued to do in Judaism. Blessings proliferated; so did exorcisms. A mentality grew favoring good deeds and abhorring evil ones which was identical with the Jewish outlook on the question. By the year 400 the "re-Judaizing" of Christianity, as it was called, was complete.

The meaning of these events has been read in diametrically opposite ways. For some, it was a tragic departure from that freedom from the Law which came with Christ. For others, it was a natural development within a church that had never gone the way of a Marcionite or gnostic spiritualism. From the fifth to the fifteenth century this nonreflexive synthesis flourished. With the Jews and the Muslims cast in the role of opponents of the gospel, the church did not examine too carefully what it had done in adopting the Jewish religion in a highly selective way. The demands of the Reformers and the response of the Catholics brought diverse answers to the question of the nature of the apostolic faith. The response given had one common factor, that the Christians were right and the Jews were wrong.

Sober reflection over the last few decades, precipitated by the methodical extermination of Europe's Jews by men and women once baptized, has brought serious changes in the Christian view of the Jewish people and God's design for them. An important task of theology not heretofore attempted has yielded some early and, one hopes, lasting results. The chief one is that Christianity's coming into being cannot be part of a divine plan to bring an end to the Jewish people and their unique role. Since the late second century, Christians have alleged, following certain NT writers, that God had held out his love to them in Christ but that the Jewish people had refused it. It is now clear that the events of the first century did not correspond to any such corporate choice on the part of Jews. Hence the comfortable Christian formulas of imputed blame are meaningless. The mystification of the NT writers over the widespread nonacceptance of Jesus by Jews is evident. Equally clear is their biblical tendency to think in categories of symbolic representation and absolute disjunction of alternatives. The exact happenings of that period are anything but evident.

It cannot be held, on any reading of the difference that Jesus made, that a divinely revealed Law lost all binding force at a certain point in history. If the covenant with Abraham and a response to it in faith is real, the Sinai dispensation cannot be less so. Jesus the Jew is believed in by Christians as a teacher sent from God to Jew and non-Jew alike. Surely he cannot be such a one at the price of bringing to an end the religious life of his people. Some early Jewish believers in him, the ones who became Christians, seem to have been unable to discern in any profound way the motives of those who did not. They resorted to charges of bad faith without analyzing other factors that might have been at work. The gentiles who followed them, as inheritors of the divine mercy, had if anything a worse record. Even Paul's attempt to cope in Rom 9–11 with a mystery that was beyond him was largely set aside, despite the germs of insight it contained.

Pat formulas were settled on instead. For the first time since Adam, God had invited people to a life like the paradisal one they had lost. God had succeeded a dispensation of law with one of grace. A free response in the spirit had taken the place of a trammeled response to the letter. The Law was described as no longer having binding force for Jews, and binding only in an ethical sense for Christians. It became synonymous with a set of works proposed by all Jews everywhere as saving in place of faith in Christ.

It seems obvious that the gracious character of the Law as an expression of covenant love has to come to the fore in Christian consciousness sooner or later. When it does, a practical corollary will be the acceptance by Christians of Jewish fidelity to God through this expression of his love. Obedience to the divine will through keeping God's commands must characterize all Christians as it did Jesus. What Jews make of Jesus—for most Christians, the only "Jewish question" there is—will then be situated where it belongs, namely, in a context of what Jews make of Christians, who are supposed to resemble Jesus.

Another corollary of recognizing the Law as a gracious gift will be that Christians will live at ease with law and custom as valid expressions of faith. To set faith against a centuries-old observance, above all against works of divine service, is to misconceive Paul utterly. The sole demand he made was that Christians acknowledge fidelity to works of the Law as the deed of God, not as the subject of a boast in a spirit independent of him.

The view just stated is not unanimous among Christian theologians. Some hold that Paul taught that all works of the

Law in fact came to an end in Christ, to be succeeded only by faith justification. But this claims too much and divides human religious response in a psychologically impossible way. It makes grace a divine gift in opposition to the human deeds that flow from it. A Law observance that is incapable of faith motivation has to be a biblical contradiction, a monster. To say that God is the author of all that is good in us (viz., an order of grace) is to say that we too are the author of all that is good in us. If we say otherwise, we do not know what it is to be human.

GRACE AS DIVINE ASSISTANCE

If an end to any opposition between law and grace is mandatory teaching for Christians, so is a division between God's work in the creation and his work of redemption. Grace is God making himself available to the creatures he has made. The act of creation is his first and enduring gift. His providential care which meant so much to Jesus is God's continued self-giving throughout the course of human life. Those who had known Christ risen declared that in him they had experienced intimacy with God on new terms. After Jesus left them, they called his intimacy the "gift of the Spirit," especially as it touched those who had not known him but accepted in faith the gift of his life, death, and resurrection for them. This is but a way to describe the divine self-disclosure. Faith is not a matter of assenting to a proposition. It is the old biblical trust in the revealing God who has done a new thing. Grace for the Christian, then, is the God of love who breathes a breath of love. But this he has always done. Viewed as God helping humanity be like him in his holiness, it is properly called a grace that elevates or sanctifies. The constant aid he gives humanity to be fully human, sometimes called in theology a "deified" life, is properly termed his assisting, cooperating, or actual grace. This is God at work making possible and easy daily obedient acts. It is his gift of providence viewed as assistance in living the life of faith.

A serious difference between Reformers and Catholics was the uneasiness of the former in the face of the latter's stress on grace as a "quality of soul." Assuming God's self-givenness to be a fact, the medieval theologians devoted much attention to created grace, as they called it, the change in humanity as a result of the relationship. Luther and others were impatient with this emphasis to the point of denying it entirely. They thought that the relationship of love and trust in a personal God was obscured by it, that the proper center which is God and not humanity was lost sight of. The fear that a change in creatures might be paramount led some Protestants to deny that any change took place. They held that God's acceptance of sinners as just was the whole reality of grace. The Catholics, in turn, less sensitive to claims for the divine graciousness than they might have been, continued to insist on the effect of the divine acceptance upon humanity. The best of their theologians, like the Reformers, stressed the personal relationship that accounted for it, but grace understood as a quality of soul succeeded in interfering with that primary teaching.

One cannot assert airily that all of those theological wars are over, for they are not. All Christians must keep pointing to the full acceptance by God of the human creature he has made from the first moment of creation. He accepts humanity even, and especially, in its condition of sin. The God who accepts and, in Paul's language, justifies is a gracious God. The result is a graced or justified condition in the race and, if there is a satisfactory human response, in the person thus accepted. This graced condition is the result of God's unconditional will that humanity be in his likeness. This, in turn, is no other than humanity's being all that it can be as human. Sin destroys this likeness by diminishing human possibilities. The sinless Jesus Christ points to what humanity can and should be. Redemption (or salvation) is God's making the restored likeness possible in Christ: from a condition of sin, never absent, to a condition of grace, likewise never absent but now in Christ fully manifest.

GRACE AND NATURE

An expression of the struggle to express the reality of grace familiar to Catholic, Orthodox, and Protestant alike is the theory of grace superadded to nature, however it may be termed. This brings us to a third opposition that must end in Christian teaching, along with those between law and grace and creation and redemption. It is not entirely distinct from either, but is another way of describing the reality of redemption. With some variety in the Christian traditions, a distinction is made between the "supernatural" and "natural" orders.

The word "supernatural" is not biblical. The closest the NT comes to it is when it speaks of the baptized as "sharers of the divine nature" (2 Pt 1:4). For the Greek fathers, the adjective "supernatural" and the phrase "above nature" described matters such as Christ's virgin birth, the gospel, and faith and the virtues. Still, these expressions never came to the fore in the East as much as in the West. The Easterners favored the term "divinization" to convey the effect on humanity of God's grace in Christ. The Latin-speaking Scotus Erigena, who translated Pseudo-Dionysius (ca. 500), and other writers of the Carolingian age fastened upon the term "supernatural" in preference to the later favorites "above nature" and "alongside nature." Aquinas brought the word "supernatural" into common use. He employed it widely, not for the miraculous or the unexplainable, but for various realities in the order of the divine saving activity and faith. From his time on, the term was common among the schoolmen to describe what Richard Hooker would later call "an advancement upon nature."[4]

Thus, from being a word of no special consequence to the

mystics, who saw all of God's work in us as befitting our nature because possible to it, "the supernatural" became the usual term for all reality in the order of grace. It included the call to conversion, the life of faith, and the beatific vision of God. Even though the Council of Trent did not use the word, it was a commonplace among Catholics and Protestants alike from the seventeenth century onward. A starting point may have been the condemnation of Michel du Baye in 1567, who held that Adam's endowments in the garden were merely "natural."[5]

In the nineteenth century the term "supernatural" continued strong in Protestant writing, but it has since fallen from favor except among conservative theologians. It was so taken for granted among Catholic theologians that the still living Henri de Lubac created a furor with his book *Surnaturel* by declaring the term a "monster" and a "sacrilege against the Creator."[6] Late medieval and post-Tridentine theologians had divided humanity, he said, creating the level of "mere nature" to which they added supernature. De Lubac holds that the human race was destined for eternal life with God by its very creation as spirit. Of this, redemption is but the continuation. Humanity has no destiny, individually and collectively, but a "supernatural one" corresponding to its desire for union with God.[7] Consequently, the term is misleading when it suggests that something finite or created is superadded to human possibility and capacity. Rather, proximity to uncreated Grace brings the human creature to its full potential.

A papal letter of 1950, *Humani Generis*, accused the French theologian of denying the gratuity of the supernatural order by his simple lesson in history. He had in fact affirmed the total gratuity of the divine plan for humanity but described it as unitary, not twofold. The vocabulary of gratuity is much a reality of the Bible. It describes God's freedom and generosity. He need not have created humanity, or chosen the Jews, or sent his son. In doing the first, however, he made a creature with a natural desire for union with himself. There was no first, "merely natural" humanity, created freely, to which a second, supernatural (non-natural?) destiny was added that required new powers and capacities—the "finite supernatural" of de Lubac's phrase. There is but one set of human powers to be brought to realization.

The medieval theologians were well aware of the problems involved here. They spoke of the passive potential in human nature (*potentia obedientiae* in Albert, Aquinas, and Bonaventure) for the vision of God, lest the discontinuity of a destiny for which humanity was unfit should assert itself. Karl Rahner has updated the medieval term by rendering it the "supernatural existential."[8] He means by this that there is in human existence a fitting proportion to God who alone is supernatural with respect to humanity. Grace is totally unmerited, even as human existence is unmerited. God does not perform gratuitous feats for us in order to elicit cravenness or gratitude. The infinite-finite distance is so great that any reflection on his goodness or the forms it takes must strike us with the magnitude of his gracious giving.

"The natural-supernatural distinction was invented for no other purpose," Charles Stinson points out, "than to glorify biblical salvation history."[9] The distinction may be helpful to remind us of the transcendent God in our lives. Its net effect, however, seems to have been to fracture the unity of the human life of spirit and provide Christian thought with a "rigid dichotomy foreign to biblical thinking."[10] God is Grace, in that he is human destiny. He is also that gracious Assistant who sees to it that humanity will come to him because he never deserts us in our need.

THE IMPORTANCE OF THIS LIFE

A final topic deserves comment. Besides Christianity's illegitimate tendency to think poorly of both created nature and covenant Law, it maintains a seeming disinterest in present human life as a result of a faith commitment to a life to come.[11] The NT teaching on the final epoch is undoubtedly responsible for this. It will not help merely to point out that Jewish eon thought is what was at stake in the first century, into which the return of Christ in glory was inserted. The subtle transfer from Jewish eon categories, with their stress on life on this earth in two stages, to the Greek concept of an immortal life with God after death, was not significant. In neither case was "this life" the matter of primary concern.

The NT imagery looked forward to a life that would be totally altered in unknown ways; the patristic alteration looked forward to an unchanging, deathless life with God in heaven. Divine judgment in the future was the watershed for both. The NT writers, being eschatologically oriented, did not have a this-worldly interest quite like that of the Jews of the Bible. But then, neither did Jews of the period generally, until the rabbis turned their attention from the nonhistorical future to the duties of the present.

To suggest that the church temper its hope in a resurrected life with Christ is scarcely a contribution. That would imperil the heart of the gospel. A legitimate demand, however, is that the sanctity of the present life be preached constantly lest God's work of creation be impugned. A French proverb says, "The better is the enemy of the good." It applies exactly in this matter. To keep repeating that the life of heaven is immeasurably better than the life of earth is to see the latter as less than good, however far this may be from what is intended.

The liturgies, the creeds, and the preaching of all the churches engage in a persistent, unconscious attack on the present work of the patient God among his responsible creatures. The language of Christianity, hoping to recall to believers a set of transcendent and eternal values, makes the interpretation of earthly existence even harder than it ordinarily would be. Subtle expressions of hope, uttered in public prayer, that the present life may soon be over or be succeeded by a much-improved existence, far from promoting the mystery of future resurrection, make religion an unreal part of human life. Faith becomes the flight from life's responsibilities that its detractors maintain it is. Such speech patterns take Christianity as far from the spirit of Jesus—whose "kingdom of heaven" was God's present reign in the midst of his people—as can be imagined.

CONCLUSIONS

The serious and inescapable realities of Christian life and doctrine that have emerged from the exploration of certain NT and patristic data in the foregoing pages include the following:

—To be faithful to Jesus Christ as the NT speaks of him is to be in full continuity with him in his Jewishness. This includes conceiving the human person-nature as a body-self unity, taking the world and the present life with utmost seriousness, and avoiding all literalist interpretations of the poetic-mythical lest its religious intent be missed entirely. The cosmos is of importance to the Christian, not as the scene of brief human testing or as something that may not be turned to idolatrous uses but as the creation of God into which humanity fits. By that fact, it is "very good."

—Praise of God as the savior of humanity is not served by the church's creating a myth of human evil followed by divine rescue. It is served only by speaking of his creation of a good humanity that will fail in the purpose he has for it unless it conforms to his will in obedience. To obey him is to let him act as savior.

—To claim that Christianity derives from the Hebrew revelation is to see the election, covenant, promises, and Law of the Jews as permanently valid. No service can be done to God by declaring his work completed by the Christian revelation which has as its result the destruction or negation of the Hebrew revelation. Christ is the end of the Law as its completion, but not as its abrogation.

—To acknowledge and accept God as gracious (or as the author of an order of grace) is to admit him as the creator,

sustainer, sanctifier, and completer of human life. The work
of God is one, but its effects are many. All of them are properly
termed "salvation," in that humanity tends to self-destruction
if it relies exclusively on its powers apart from him.

—To accept the Hebrew Scriptures is to believe in an order
of grace in which the Jews were implicated but which did not
exhaust the divine goodness. That God was gracious to other
peoples the believer in the Bible assumes, but exactly how he
was gracious the believer cannot know. Since the Mosaic Law
is one means of grace and the death and resurrection of Jesus
Christ another, the two cannot be mutually exclusive. A certain outlook on the Law may vitiate it, as may the same outlook on the cross. Obedient acceptance of God's will means
that the Law will have a place in Christian faith forever.

—To hold, as the church does, that the same God is the author
of both testaments is to require exploration of the opposition
to all things Jewish that has marked it from the beginning. A
community of faith that requires the negation of another faith
to achieve its identity is unworthy of a God of justice and love.

The Bible is a vast body of literature that contains a message of hope. Extracting certain themes from it has resulted
in a variety of Judaisms and Christianities. The tendency to
select and interpret is inevitable. Rabbinism, mysticism, hasi-
dism, churches, creeds, and the practice of oracular quota-
tion all testify to this. The manifestations of the tendency are
many more.

These pages ask but one thing: that Christians in community be true to their oldest tradition and call upon the Spirit
to help them select and interpret well. They must extract
from the rich treasures of religious language they possess
those affirmations of God and world (all nature graced) and
the Jews and Jesus Christ (covenant Law obeyed lovingly,
trustingly) that most befit a responsible humanity before a
holy God.

NOTES

INTRODUCTION

1. Among studies on the Jewish origins of Christianity are Jean Daniélou, *The Theology of Jewish Christianity* (London: Darton, Longman & Todd, 1964; Philadelphia: The Westminster Press, 1977); H. J. Schoeps, *Theologie und Geschichte des Judenchristentums* (Tübingen: J. C. B. Mohr [Paul Siebeck], 1949); H. J. Schoeps, *Jewish Christianity* (Fortress Press, 1969).

2. Some helpful titles would include Arnold J. Toynbee (ed.), *The Crucible of Christianity* (The World Publishing Co., 1969); Henry Chadwick, *The Early Church* (Penguin Books, 1967); Robert M. Grant, *Augustus to Constantine* (Harper & Row, 1970); Robert A. Markus, *Christianity in the Roman World* (London: Thames & Hudson, 1974). For a philosophical treatment of the ideas current in the early centuries of Christianity, see Arthur H. Armstrong and Robert A. Markus, *Christian Faith and Greek Philosophy* (Sheed & Ward, 1960); Jean Daniélou, *Gospel Message and Hellenistic Culture* (The Westminster Press, 1973).

3. The Bible passages are the author's own translation. Chapter and verse numbers are those of *The New American Bible* (The Catholic Press, 1970).

4. Irenaeus' contention against the proponents of *"gnōsis* falsely so called," to whom he addressed a work in five books about the year 175, was that the world of matter and time was not alien to humanity nor to be rejected as hostile to it. God "made temporal things for the sake of man, that by means of them he might grow to maturity and bear fruit for immortality" (*Against Heresies* IV, 5, 1). History was therefore real and important but at the same time a kind of proving ground for the mature existence to be lived in a deathless condition. Cf. Daniélou, *Gospel Message and Hellenistic Culture,* pp. 387–425.

5. A good summary of this situation is to be found in Roger Gryson, *Les Origines du célibat ecclésiastique* (Gembloux: J. Duculot, 1970). Cf. J. N. D. Kelly, *Jerome: His Life, Writings, and Controversies* (Harper & Row, 1976), pp. 179–194 and *passim*.

6. For the development of this mentality in Christian thought, see Charles Stinson, "The Finite Supernatural: Theological Perspectives," *Religious Studies* 9 (Sept. 1973), 325–337.

Chapter I
DELIVERANCE AND TORAH

1. Cf. R. H. Charles (ed.), *The Apocrypha and Pseudepigrapha of the Old Testament*, 2 vols. (Oxford: Clarendon Press, 1913); also Martin Hengel, *Judaism and Hellenism: Studies in Their Encounter in Palestine During the Early Hellenistic Period*, 2 vols. (Fortress Press, 1975).

2. Josephus, *Life* 2; Josephus, *Jewish War* II, 8, 2–13; Philo (Essenes), cf. *Quod omnis probus liber* XII–XIII; *Hypothetica* 11.1–18; *De vita contemplativa* (on the Therapeutae), II, 13.

3. On this question, cf. Walter Schmithals, *Paul and the Gnostics* (Abingdon Press, 1972), including a table of all the polemical and apologetic passages in Paul's epistles, pp. 243f.

4. Yehezkel Kaufmann, *The Religion of Israel: From Its Beginnings to the Babylonian Exile,* tr. by Moshe Greenberg (Schocken Books, 1972), p. 63.

5. "One must be careful to note, however, that [the LORD] intervened only when the enemies of his people would otherwise have been insuperable" (Jacob M. Myers, *Grace and Torah* [Fortress Press, 1975], p. 9). This chapter is much indebted to the insights of Myers' book. Throughout the telling of the biblical story in the chapter, its character as *mythos* is assumed. At no point are modern questions of historicity raised. The only "scientific" considerations are those of the intent and inner coherence of the tales.

6. Otto Eissfeldt, *The Old Testament: An Introduction* (Harper & Row, 1965), p. 195; cf. Moshe Greenberg, "The Redaction of the Plague Narrative in Exodus," in Hans Goedicke (ed.), *Near Eastern Studies: In Honor of William Foxwell Albright* (The Johns Hopkins Press, 1971), pp. 243–252, for a theory of the interweaving of the earlier (JE) and later (P) elements.

7. Abraham J. Heschel, *The Prophets* (Harper & Row, 1962), p. 230.

8. *Ibid.*

9. W. F. Lofthouse makes the claim that "mercy" *(ḥesed)* is used

only where there is some recognized tie or claim, whereas "grace" (ḥen) is a word of utter gratuity where no such claim exists. Cf. "ḥen and ḥesed in the OT," *Zeitschrift für die alttestamentliche Wissenschaft* 51 (1933), 29, 33.

10. Hans Werner Wolff, "The Day of Rest in the Old Testament," *Lexington Theological Quarterly* 7 (1962), 65–76.

11. Julius Wellhausen, *Sketch of the History of Israel and Judah*, 2d ed. (London: A. & C. Black, 1891), p. 88; cf. p. 19.

12. Walther Eichrodt, "Prophet and Covenant: Observations on the Exegesis of Isaiah," in J. Durham and J. Porter (eds.), *Proclamation and Presence: Old Testament Essays in Honour of G. H. Davies* (London: SCM Press, 1970), p. 167.

13. See George Mendenhall, *Law and Covenant in Israel and the Ancient Near East* (Pittsburgh: The Biblical Colloquium, 1955), p. 46.

14. Cf. M. Weidenfeld, *Deuteronomy and the Deuteronomic School* (Oxford: Clarendon Press, 1972).

15. Edmund Jacob, *Theology of the Old Testament* (London: Hodder & Stoughton, 1958), p. 274.

16. For a discussion and bibliography on this question, see Robert Banks, *Jesus and the Law in the Synoptic Tradition* (Cambridge University Press, 1975), pp. 27f.

17. Cf. William F. Arndt and F. Wilbur Gingrich (tr. of Walter Bauer), *A Greek-English Lexicon of the New Testament and Other Early Christian Literature* (The University of Chicago Press, 1957), p. 182.

18. Banks, *Jesus and the Law in the Synoptic Tradition*, pp. 32ff.

19. Cf. David Daube, *The New Testament and Rabbinic Judaism* (London: Athlone Press, 1956), pp. 275–282.

20. Cf. Donald Juel, *Messiah and Temple: The Trial of Jesus in the Gospel of Mark* (Missoula: Society of Biblical Literature, 1977).

Chapter II
THE LAW IN THE TEACHING OF JESUS

1. *The Gospel According to Thomas*, Coptic text est. and tr. by A. Guillaumont *et al.* (Harper & Brothers, 1959).

2. Howard Clark Kee, *Jesus in History*, 2d rev. ed. (Harcourt, Brace and World, 1977), pp. 88f.

3. Walter Schmithals, *Paul and James* (London: SCM Press, 1965), p. 109.

4. Cf. Victor Paul Furnish, *The Love Command in the New Testament* (Abingdon Press 1972), pp. 25–30, 74.

5. Jack T. Sanders, *Ethics in the New Testament* (Fortress Press, 1975), p. 32.

6. Sanders in his stress on Mark's church as an eschatological community omits mention of the phrase, "wherever the gospel is proclaimed throughout the world" (Mk 14:9), and reduces Jesus' teaching on divorce (10:2–12) to a saying proper to an eschatological society. He omits all mention of the presence in Mark of six commandments of the ten (10:19) except as part of a discussion of the similarity of Matthew's wording of the same passage (Mt 19:18f., esp. v. 19*b*) to Paul's (Rom 13:9); this against the phrasing of Mk 10: 19 and Lk 18:20, which do not add, "Love your neighbor as yourself." Presumably Sanders holds that the entire decalogue yields in Mark to Jesus' eschatological teaching: "Go and sell what you have and give to the poor" (Mk 10:21). This fits in with his theory that the historical Jesus gave no ethical teaching proper to this age but only commands impossible of fulfillment in it, such as the behavior of the good Samaritan (Lk 10:29–37), a parable found in Luke only. To make it bear the weight he does, as typical of unfulfillable behavior short of immediate anticipation of the final age, Sanders must omit mention of Jesus' reply to the lawyer's recital of Dt 6:5 and Lv 19: 18 (Lk 10:27): "Do this and you shall live" (Lk 10:28). This saying makes sense only if the lawyer could and should keep those high points of the Law.

7. Cf. John R. Donahue, *Are You the Christ? The Trial Narrative in the Gospel of Mark*, SBL Dissertation Series 10 (Missoula: Society of Biblical Literature, 1973), pp. 168–171, 221–224.

8. Cf. Günther Bornkamm, "End-Expectation and Church in Matthew," in Günther Bornkamm, Gerhard Barth, and Heinz Joachim Held, *Tradition and Interpretation in Matthew* (The Westminster Press, 1963), p. 24.

9. 1 QS i, 10 (cf. Ps 139:21f.).

10. Bornkamm, in Bornkamm, Barth, and Held, *Tradition and Interpretation in Matthew*, p. 29.

11. Cf. George F. Moore, *Judaism in the First Centuries of the Christian Era and the Age of the Tannaim*, Vol. I (Harvard University Press, 1927), pp. 251–262; cf. *Pirqe Aboth* I, 1.

12. Douglas R. A. Hare and Daniel Harrington, in "Make Disciples of All the Gentiles (Mt 28:19)," *Catholic Biblical Quarterly* 37, 3 (July 1975), 359–369, hold that Israel and the gentiles are the distinct entities of salvation history for Matthew. They maintain that the phrase *panta ta 'ethnē* of Matthew's final "missionary command" was directed by him to the gentiles only, against W. Trilling, *Das wahre Israel* (1964) and B. J. Hubbard (1974), who think that in the plural *ta 'ethnē* includes Israel.

13. Ernst Käsemann, *New Testament Questions of Today* (Fortress Press, 1969), "Sentences of Holy Law in the New Testament," p. 79.

14. *Ibid.*, p. 78.

15. *Ibid.*, p. 80. This essay speaks of God's remaining God "even when he becomes gracious to us" *(ibid.)*. It holds the view that the realm of holy law is abandoned in all church law, a tendency observable as early as the NT. "The Spirit is now only the power of obedience inasmuch as he creates order in the community" (p. 81). The author pleads for something less horizontal and more vertical—namely, law oriented toward the Last Day and grounded in it. He is supported by Matthew in his emphasis on the judgment, and a church that followed Matthew in his eschatological concern through *praxis* (Mt 16:27).

16. Cf. Hans Conzelmann, *The Theology of St. Luke* (Harper & Row, 1961), pp. 145ff., 232; G. Haenchen, *The Acts of the Apostles* (The Westminster Press, 1971); G. Barth, in Bornkamm, Barth, and Held, *Tradition and Interpretation in Matthew*, p. 63.

17. Jacob Jervell, *Luke and the People of God: A New Look at Luke-Acts* (Augsburg Publishing House, 1972), esp. "The Law in Luke-Acts," pp. 133–151.

18. Thus Joseph Fitzmyer, who qualifies the notion by saying that "Acts vaguely suggests that the Christian group looked on itself as the New Israel." Cf. "Jewish Christianity in Acts in Light of the Qumrân Scrolls," in *Essays on the Semitic Background of the New Testament*, Sources for Biblical Study 5 (Missoula: Society of Biblical Literature and Scholars Press, 1974), p. 275; the essay first appeared in L. E. Keck and J. L. Martyn (eds.), *Studies in Luke-Acts* (Abingdon Press, 1966), pp. 233–257. Fitzmyer does not enter into the questions of the historical character of the account in Acts or the author's theology as redactive principle. He does assume with Gärtner, speaking of Luke's Jerusalem Christians and the Qumrân group, that, "In both we find a kindred idea that the Jerusalem temple and its sacrificial cultus have been replaced by a community of the faithful" (p. 295). Cf. Bertil Gärtner, *The Temple and the Community in Qumrân and the New Testament*, SNTS Monograph Series 1 (Cambridge University Press, 1965), pp. 99–101.

19. Cf. Jervell, *Luke and the People of God,* p. 139.

20. *Ibid.*, p. 142.

21. *Ibid.*, p. 145. Jervell here takes issue with Conzelmann's view in *The Theology of St. Luke* that "the Law is given up in principle by the Church (Acts XV, 28f.)," p. 147; cf. pp. 212f.

22. Stephen G. Wilson, *The Gentiles and the Gentile Mission in Luke-Acts* (Cambridge University Press, 1973), p. 246.

23. *Ibid.*

24. *Ibid.*, p. 248.

25. Cf. Jervell, *Luke and the People of God,* "The Divided People of God," p. 64.

26. Robert Banks, *Jesus and the Law in the Synoptic Tradition,* p. 238.

27. *Ibid.*, p. 242.

28. *Ibid.*, p. 252.

29. *Ibid.*, p. 243.

30. Cf. John Knox, *The Ethic of Jesus in the Teaching of the Church* (Abingdon Press, 1961).

31. *Ibid.*, pp. 60f.

32. *Ibid.*, p. 60.

33. *Ibid.*, p. 48.

Chapter III
Is Christ the End of the Law?

1. J. A. Ziesler, *The Meaning of Righteousness in Paul* (Cambridge University Press, 1972), p. 165.

2. *Ibid.*, p. 169.

3. Cf. Robert G. Hamerton-Kelly, *Pre-existence, Wisdom, and the Son of Man,* SNTS Monograph Series 21 (Cambridge University Press, 1973), p. 6, against Rudolf Bultmann, *Theology of the New Testament,* Vol. I (Charles Scribner's Sons, 1952), pp. 304f.; for Bultmann's predominant concern with Paul's Christ as savior of humanity, cf. Vol. I, pp. 176, 191, 228ff.

4. J. G. Gibbs, "The Cosmic Scope of Redemption According to Paul," *Biblica* 56, 1 (1975), 25. Cf. Gibbs's *Creation and Redemption: A Study in Pauline Theology* (Leiden: Brill, 1971), pp. 100f.

5. Gibbs, *Creation and Redemption,* p. 149.

6. *Ibid.*, p. 142; cf. p. 134.

7. Ernst Käsemann, *Perspectives on Paul* (London: SCM Press, 1971), "On Paul's Anthropology," p. 8.

8. Rudolf Bultmann, *Existence and Faith,* tr. by Schubert M. Ogden (Meridian Books, 1960), "Paul," p. 126. German original, "Paulus," *RGG²,* IV. 1019–1045.

9. Cf. Robin Scroggs, *The Last Adam* (Fortress Press, 1966), "Adam in Rabbinic Literature," pp. 32–58.

10. Käsemann, *Perspectives on Paul,* p. 18.

11. *Ibid.*, p. 26.

12. Cf. Elaine Pagels, *The Gnostic Paul* (Fortress Press, 1975), for

the data on their exegesis. Professor Pagels is by no means sure that the church rejected it.

13. Cf. E. A. Speiser, *Genesis,* The Anchor Bible (Doubleday & Co., 1964), p. 26; J. L. McKenzie, "The Literary Characteristics of Genesis 2–3," *Theological Studies* 15 (1954), 562f.

14. Cf. W. D. Davies, *Paul and Rabbinic Judaism* (Harper & Row, Harper Torchbooks, 1965), pp. 38f.; cf. Scroggs, *The Last Adam,* pp. 32–38; Philo, *De mundi opificio* 135–152.

15. Cf. G. B. Caird, *Principalities and Powers* (Oxford University Press, 1956).

16. Cf. E. P. Sanders, "Patterns of Religion in Paul and Rabbinic Judaism: A Holistic Method of Comparison," *Harvard Theological Review* 66, 4 (Oct. 1973), 478. Sanders thinks Ziesler, *The Meaning of Righteousness in Paul,* wrong in supposing that the noun and adjective forms of the *dikai-* word group (e.g., in Gal 2:15–21) tend to describe ethical renewal and the verb forms forgiveness or a right relation with God.

17. For copious support of this statement, see Arthur Marmorstein, *The Doctrine of Merits in Old Rabbinic Literature* (KTAV, 1968), pp. 12–15. Marmorstein seems to think that divine election and human merit were held by opposite schools.

18. Sanders cites R. Mach, *Der Zaddik in Talmud und Midrasch* (Leiden: Brill, 1967), on being "righteous" in rabbinic Judaism.

19. Cf. Myers, *Grace and Torah,* p. 67, citing J. J. Scullion, "Sedeq-Sedaqah in Isaiah cc. 40–66," in *Ugarit-Forschungen* 3 (Kevelaer: Verlag Butzon & Bercker, 1971), pp. 335–348.

20. Augustine, *Enchir.* 99–101; Calvin, *Inst.*

Chapter IV
BEYOND THE SYNOPTICS AND PAUL

1. Josephus, *Antiquities* XX, 200.

2. W. G. Kümmel, *Introduction to the New Testament,* rev. ed. (Abingdon Press, 1975), pp. 405f. For a more extended commentary on James, see that of the present author in Gerhard A. Krodel (ed.), *Hebrews, James, 1 and 2 Peter, Jude, Revelation,* Proclamation Commentary Series (Fortress Press, 1977).

3. A. Meyer, *Das Rätsel des Jakobs,* Supplement, *Zeitschrift für die neutestamentliche Wissenschaft* 10 (1930), cited by Kümmel, *Introduction to the New Testament.*

4. Cf. Leander E. Keck, "The Poor Among the Saints in the NT," *Zeitschrift für die neutestamentliche Wissenschaft* 56 (1965), 108ff.

5. Donald Guthrie, *New Testament Introduction* (Inter-Varsity Press, 1970).

6. C. K. Barrett, *The Gospel of John and Judaism* (Fortress Press, 1975), p. 71.

7. Werner Elert, *Law and Gospel,* tr. by E. H. Schroeder (Fortress Press, 1967), p. 18.

8. Cf. Ignace de la Potterie, "*Charis* paulinienne et *charis* johannique," E. E. Ellis and E. Grasser (eds.), *Paulus und Jesus* (Göttingen: Vandenhoeck & Ruprecht, 1975), pp. 256, 260.

9. *Ibid.,* pp. 270–276.

10. For the philosophical arguments in favor of rendering *anti* in this way, and the absence of any other usage from the period, cf. *ibid.,* p. 261, n. 19; p. 263, n. 25.

11. Cf. Pagels, *The Gnostic Paul,* pp. 157–164, where this point is well made in summary.

Chapter V
GRECO-ROMAN INFLUENCES

1. Arthur D. Nock thinks otherwise: "Any idea that what we call the Christian sacraments were in their origin indebted to pagan mysteries or even to the metaphysical concepts based upon them shatters on the rock of linguistic evidence" (Arthur D. Nock, *Early Gentile Christianity and Its Hellenistic Background* [Harper & Row, Harper Torchbooks, 1964], "Hellenistic Mysteries and Christian Sacraments," p. 132).

2. Apuleius, *The Golden Ass* XI, 22.

3. Arthur D. Nock, *Conversion: The Old and the New in Religion from Alexander the Great to Augustine of Hippo* (Oxford: Clarendon Press, 1933), esp. Chs. 6, 7, 8. Nock maintains that much adherence to deities and cults precisely did *not* imply conversion but merely popular devotion; cf. A. J. Festugière, *Personal Religion Among the Greeks* (University of California Press, 1954), esp. pp. 75–84, 89–91, 95–104, for examples of feelings of intimacy between devotee and deity.

4. Martin Hengel, *The Son of God: The Origin of Christology and the History of Jewish-Hellenistic Religion* (Fortress Press, 1976), follows Carsten Colpe, *Die religionsgeschichtliche Schule,* Forschungen zur Religion und Literatur des Alten und Neuen Testaments 78 (Göttingen: Vandenhoeck & Ruprecht, 1961), in maintaining that, whereas a gnostic spirit preceded Christianity, it was Christ the redeemer of the Christians who provided the basis for the myth.

5. Eric R. Dodds, *Pagan and Christian in an Age of Anxiety* (W. W. Norton & Co., 1970). Dodds follows the line taken by Arthur D. Nock in his essay "Gnosticism," in Zeph Stewart (ed.), *Essays on Religion and the Ancient World*, Vol. II (Harvard University Press, 1972), pp. 940–959, which does not find the claim of the Persian origins of the gnostic dualist spirit persuasive.

6. John Philoponus (the Grammarian) is the thinker who denied the special equation of "celestial" with "divine." Cf. Samuel Sambursky, *The Physical World of Late Antiquity* (London: Routledge & Kegan Paul, 1962), Ch. 6.

7. Plato, *Timaeus* 92C.

8. *Ibid.*, 29E, 30A.

9. Cf. John Bowker, *The Targums and Rabbinic Literature* (Cambridge University Press, 1969), pp. 125f.; Louis Ginzberg, *The Legends of the Jews*, Vol. I (Jewish Publication Society of America, 1909), pp. 71–75, 94f.

10. On the rejection of the "two powers" or "two authorities," cf. Moore, *Judaism in the First Centuries of the Christian Era and the Age of the Tannaim*, Vol. I, pp. 364–367; Yehezkel Kaufmann provides reasons why Jewish demonology located evil in the moral realm, never the metaphysical, in *The Religion of Israel*, pp. 63–67.

11. Robert C. Zaehner (ed.), *The Concise Encyclopedia of Living Faiths* (Beacon Press, 1967), p. 209.

12. Nock, in "The Problem of Zoroaster," maintains that a rudimentary dualism existed independently of Zoroaster, who probably opposed a contemporary worship of Mithra while finding certain ethical aspects of that cult to his purpose. Cf. "The Problem of Zoroaster," in Stewart (ed.), *Essays on Religion and the Ancient World*, Vol. II, pp. 682–702.

13. On this enthusiasm for abstention from marriage, cf. the apocryphal Acts of Thomas 13f., 124, in Edgar Hennecke and Wilhelm Schneemelcher (eds.), *New Testament Apocrypha*, Vol. II: *Writings Related to the Apostles; Apocalypses and Related Subjects* (The Westminster Press, 1966), pp. 449f., 508f.; for the horror in which adultery and fornication were held, see the Apocalypse of Peter, *ibid.*, pp. 672f.; see Bernard Cooke, *Ministry to Word and Sacraments* (Fortress Press, 1976), pp. 14–15, 545.

14. Rudolf Bultmann is the best-known protagonist of a pre-Christian gnosticism in a strict sense. Cf. his works *Primitive Christianity in Its Contemporary Setting* (Meridian Books, 1956), pp. 167–176; *Theology of the New Testament*, Vol. I (Charles Scribner's Sons, 1955), pp. 164–183.

Chapter VI
THE CHURCH FATHERS SET THE COURSE

1. Cf. Justin, *1 Apology* 43. On the tradition of the fathers of responsibility in opposition to fatalism, see Jaroslav Pelikan, *The Emergence of the Catholic Tradition (100–600)* (The University of Chicago Press, 1971), pp. 278–285.

2. Cf. Origen, *On Prayer* 6, 29, 13; cf. also Augustine, *City of God* 5, 9.

3. Origen, *Against Celsus* 5, 21.

4. Tatian, *Discourse Against the Greeks* 11.

5. Irenaeus, *Against Heresies* IV, 39, 3.

6. Thomas F. Torrance, *The Doctrine of Grace in the Apostolic Fathers* (Edinburgh: Oliver & Boyd, 1948), p. 133.

7. *Ibid.*, p. 136. "There was not a great deal of difference between a degenerate Judaism and the best ethic of Stoicism, and the transition from Hellenism to Judaism was therefore much easier than to a full orbed Christianity with its Gospel of grace" (p. 137).

8. Epistle of Barnabas 12, 5.

9. Hermas, Shepherd, *Mandatum* xii, I–VI. James (1:14 and 4:1) likewise appears to hold this theory.

10. *Ibid.*, III, 5.

11. Justin, *Dialogue with Trypho,* ch. 94: "He declared by this that he is dissolving the power of the serpent, who caused the sin done by Adam to come about, and to those who believed in him who was destined to be killed by this sign, that is by the cross, he declared salvation from the bites of the serpent, which are evil deeds, idolatry and other wrongdoing." Cf. also ch. 100.

12. *Ibid.*, ch. 95. The Jews under the Law are cursed according to Dt 27:26 because they have not scrupulously observed everything, the gentiles far more so because they commit idolatry and homosexuality and indulge in other evil practices.

13. Justin, *1 Apology* 28: "In the beginning he made the race of men endowed with intelligence, able to choose the truth and do right, so that all are without excuse before God, for they were made with the powers of reason and observation."

14. Justin, *Dialogue with Trypho,* ch. 88: "He [endures the experience of birth and crucifixion] for the sake of the human race who ever since Adam's time had fallen under the power of death and of the serpent's deceit, as each person committed sin on his own responsibility. God . . . arranged that if [those angels and men who had free will and the power of self-direction] should choose to do what

was pleasing to him he would preserve them immune from corruption and punishment, but if they behaved wickedly he would punish each as seemed best to him."

15. Irenaeus, *Against Heresies* V, 19, 1; 21. Cf. Tertullian, *On the Flesh of Christ* 17.

16. Theophilus, *To Autolycus* 2, 29.

17. Epistle of Barnabas 1, 2.

18. Ignatius, *To the Magnesians* 8, 2.

19. Justin, *2 Apology* 13; cf. Jas 1:21.

20. *1 Clement* VII, 6 and 7.

21. Basil, *Epistle* 38, 4. Elsewhere Basil speaks of this as the initial grace, whereby God created man in his likeness (*Ascetical Sermon* 1).

22. John Chrysostom, *On the Ascension* 4.

23. Origen, *On First Principles* I, 3, 6.

24. Dodds, *Pagan and Christian in an Age of Anxiety,* p. 137.

25. E. W. Watson, in W. T. Whitley (ed.), *The Doctrine of Grace* (The Macmillan Company, n. d.), p. 111. The volume is a report to the Faith and Order Movement submitted in August, 1931.

26. So Augustine was convinced that Pelagius' thought could be summarized. Cf. Augustine, *On the Grace of Christ* 35, 38.

27. Augustine, *Incomplete Work against Julian* 2. 74; cf. *ibid.,* 1. 78.

28. Augustine, *On the Proceedings of Pelagius* 11, 23; *On Original Sin* 11, 12. The Council of Orange (529) condemned these propositions among a total of twenty-five, largely accepting Augustine's wording.

29. Cf. Irenaeus, *Presentation [Demonstration] of the Apostolic Preaching,* chs. 12–18, 31–33. This treatise also tells (ch. 18) of the sin of the angels on the basis of 1 En 6:2; 7:1.

30. Cf. Irenaeus, *Against Heresies* V, 2, 1; V, 6, 1; V, 16, 13.

31. Cf. Tatian, *On Prayer* 7.

32. Theophilus, *To Autolycus* 2, 24f., 27.

33. Irenaeus, *Against Heresies* IV, 62. The view is repeated in 63, 1; cf. *Presentation,* ch. 12.

34. Irenaeus, *Against Heresies* V, 6, 1.

35. *Ibid.,* IV, 64, 1.

36. *Ibid.,* IV, 69, 2.

37. Augustine, *Confessions* 1, 4.

38. *Ibid.,* 4, 12.

39. Augustine, *On Nature and Grace* 32, 36; cf. 29, 33.

40. Augustine, *Confessions* 13, 5, 11.

41. Cf. Augustine, *Enchiridion* 8, 26f.; *City of God* 13, 4f.; 14; *On Rebuke and Grace* 12, 33.

42. Augustine, *Enchiridion* 9, 30.

43. Augustine, *Confessions* IV, 12, 18.

44. Augustine, *Enchiridion* 22, 107.

45. Augustine, *On Rebuke and Grace* 2, 3.

46. Faustus of Riez, *On Grace* 1, 13.

47. John Cassian, *Conferences* 13, 1.

48. Augustine, *On Rebuke and Grace* XIV, 44 (ML44, 943).

49. Augustine, *Enchiridion* 27, 103.

50. As quoted by Prosper of Aquitaine, *Response to the Objections of the Gauls* 1, 8.

51. Faustus of Riez, *On Grace* 1, 16.

52. Prosper of Aquitaine, *Against [Cassian] the Lecturer* 12, 4.

53. Faustus of Riez, *On Grace* 2, 10.

54. Pelikan, *The Emergence of the Catholic Tradition (100–600)*, p. 324.

55. Prosper of Aquitaine, *Response to the Genoese* 3.

Chapter VII
IMPLICATIONS FOR CONTEMPORARY FAITH

1. H. Denzinger and A. Schönmetzer, *Enchiridion Symbolorum*, 32d ed. (Freiburg: Herder, 1963), 800f. [428f.], pp. 259f.; English translation from the Latin available in John H. Leith (ed.), *Creeds of the Churches* (Doubleday Anchor Books, 1963), pp. 57f.

2. Denzinger and Schönmetzer, 790–797 [420–427], pp. 255–258.

3. Robin Scroggs, in *Paul for a New Day* (Fortress Press, 1977), has correlated the Pauline teaching in eschatological terms with modern psychoanalytical teaching: "The passage from one world to the next does not destroy the authentic self. Rather it destroys the pseudo-self created by the project of self-justification and thus allows the genuine self, that human person intended by God, actually to come into existence" (p. 20).

4. Richard Hooker, *On the Laws of Ecclesiastical Polity* 5, 56, 6. The first five of its eight books appeared in his lifetime in the 1590's. William Law wrote in his *Serious Call to a Devout and Holy Life* (1728): "Christianity supposes, intends, desires, aims at nothing else but the raising fallen man to a Divine life, to such habits of holiness, such degrees of devotion, as may fit him to enter amongst the holy inhabitants of the kingdom of heaven" (Chapter XIV, end). (Everyman's Library, 91; London: J. M. Dent & Sons, 1955, p. 184.)

5. Cf. Denzinger-Bannwart-Rahner, 30th ed. (1954), 1023 and 1021.

6. Henri de Lubac, *Surnaturel* (Paris: Aubier, 1946), p. 486.

7. *Ibid.,* p. 394.

8. Karl Rahner, *Theological Investigations,* Vol. I (Baltimore: Helicon Press, 1961), 312n.

9. Charles Stinson, "The Finite Supernatural: Theological Perspectives," *Religious Studies* 9 (Sept. 1973), 335.

10. *Ibid.*

11. The expression of this mentality by William Law should adequately represent all the major faith traditions: "Most of the employments of life are in their own nature lawful; and all those that are so may be made a substantial part of our duty to God, if we engage in them only so far and for such ends, as are suitable to beings that are to live above the world, all the time that they live in the world. This is the only measure of our application to any worldly business, let it be what it will, where it will; it must have no more of our hands, our hearts, or our time, than is consistent with a hearty, daily, careful preparation of ourselves for another life. For as all Christians, as such have renounced this world, to prepare themselves . . . for an eternal state of quite another nature, they must look upon worldly employments, as . . . things not to be desired but only to be endured and suffered, till death and resurrection have carried us to an eternal state of real happiness." (William Law, *A Serious Call to a Devout and Holy Life,* pp. 36f.)

SCRIPTURE INDEX

JEWISH SCRIPTURES AND RELATED WRITINGS

Genesis
1:1–2. 20
1:26 155
1:27 51
1:28 155
1:31 23
1–11. 21
2:1–3. 27
2:7 155
2:18–24 . . 23,155
2:20 . . . . . 23, 90
2:24 51
2:25 90
3 . . . . . 19, 140
3:5 21
3:7, 16–19, 22ff. 90
3:20 155
4:1–16. 21
4:7 89
5:2 51
6:1–4. 21
6:4 19
6:5f. 21
8:21f. 23
9:13–17 23
12 23
12:2f., 7 23
12:3 61
13:14–17 23

15:1, 5f., 8 . . . 23
15:6 . . . . . 96, 97
15:17–21 24
16:15 17
17:1–8, 9–14,
  23–27. 24
17:16 17
17:17f. 25
21:2 17
22:17f. 24
25:23 24
27:27ff. 24
32:29 24
35:10, 11f., 15 . 24
47:28 24
49:8–12 24
50:24 24

Exodus
3:1 22
3:5f. 24
3:12 22
3:14 25
4:14ff., 28, 29f. . 22
4:20 22
4:25 24
5:1 22
5:2, 10–13, 21 . 22
6:1 22

6:2ff., 7*a* 24
6:7*b*–8. 25
9:16 102
12:24, 27 22
13:21 17
14:19–22 17
16:4–35 17
17:6 17
19:5–6. 25
20:2, 2–17. . . . 26
21:24 51
22:19 21
30:13 51
33:19 102
34:33ff. 17
38:26 51

Leviticus
13–14 51
17–18 62
17–26 32
18:16 51
19:13 51
19:18 . . 45, 111f.
20:21 51
24:20 51

Numbers
14:16 17

198

SCRIPTURE INDEX

15:37 51
20:7–11 17
28:10 46
35:30 119

Deuteronomy
5:6 . . . . . . 26, 31
5:15 27
6:4f. . . 45, 46, 121
6:20ff. 31
10:12ff. 31
12–26 31
17:6 119
19:15 . . . 52, 119
19:21 51
24 47
24:1, 15 51
26:5ff. 31
27:26 . . . 74, 111
28–30 31
30:20 27
32:47 27

Joshua
2:14 117

1 Samuel
28:13 21

2 Samuel
2:6 117
7:16 28
15:20 117
23:5 28

2 Kings
22:10f. 30
22:13 31
23:3 31

1 Chronicles
16:14ff. 32
17:21f. 32
21:1 128

2 Chronicles
6:5 32
7:22 32
30:6 32
33:8 32
34:32a 31

Ezra
7:10, 26 32
9:12 33
10:44 33

Nehemiah
1:7ff. 33
8 33
10:8 32
10:29ff. 33
12 33
13:8 32
13:15–22, 23–30 33

Tobit
4:10f. 35
12:8f. 35

Job
1:6 128
2:1 19
23:12 34
26:7 20

Psalms
5:10 95
8:3–8. 11
10:7 95
14:1ff. 95
36:2 95
66:16ff. 119
78:49 19
85:11 117
100:3–5 11
109:7 119
119:73. 11
136. 23

140:4 95
148, 150. . . . 156

Proverbs
1:8 34
1:16 95
3:1 34
10:12 110
13:14 34
15:8 34
15:29 119
19:16 34
21:7 34
28:4–7 34
29:18 34

Ecclesiastes
8:2, 5 34
12:13 34

Wisdom of Solomon
2:12 34
2:24 . . . 128, 139
6:4 34
11–19 34

Sirach
2:15f. 34
7:27–31 34
35:1 34
45 34
49:4 34

Isaiah
1:4 30
1:15 . . . . 30, 119
5:7, 8 30
6:9f. 54
14:10–15 . . 90
53:1 . . 103
55:3 . 31
59:7 95
59:20f. 102
61:8 31

Jeremiah
31:34 31

Baruch
2:19 35

Ezekiel
11:19 32
28:2, 6. 90

Daniel
3:23 156

Hosea
4:2, 17. 30
7:1, 4a. 30
8:4 30
13:2 30

Amos
3:2 31
8:5 30
9:11f. 61

Micah
2:1f. 30
7:6 30

Zephaniah
3:4 30

Zechariah
3:1 128

1 Maccabees
1:57 34
2:20f., 27 34
2:50ff. 34

2 Maccabees
1:2ff. 34
7:37 35

Test. of Naphtali
8:5 35

Test. of Levi
13:5 35

Asmp. of Moses
12:6–7, 10–11 . 35

2 Baruch
14:7 35
51:7 35

2 Esdras
9:7 35

CHRISTIAN SCRIPTURES AND RELATED WRITINGS

Matthew
1:19 53
1:22 51
2:15 51
3:15 50
4:8 129
5 77
5–7. 111
5:7 53
5:17–19 . . . 49, 66
5:18–19, 20,
   21, 22, 23 . . 50
5:19 55
5:20, 27, 48. . . 49
5:22–26, 28–30,
   34–37. 52
5:29 130
5:32, 39–42. . . 53
5:33–37 52
5:37 108

6:1–18 52
6:14 55
7:1, 7ff., 24ff. . . 108
7:15ff. 50
7:22 55
8:4 51
8:10, 13 53
8:11f. 54
9:2, 22, 28f. . . . 53
9:13 53
9:20 51
10:5f., 17f. . . . 54
10:23 54
10:41f. 53
12:7 53
12:15 46
12:26 51
13:11–15, 13 . . 54
13:17 53
13:52 52

14:4 51
14:36 51
15:2, 6, 11,
   18–20, ... 53
15:3, 6, 9, 14. . 52
15:12, 13, 14. . 54
16:6, 11 52
16:27 187
17:24 51
18:15–18 52
18:33 53
19:18f. 46
21:43 54
22:7f. 54
22:34–40 45
22:37ff. . . . 46, 66
23:2, 3f. 52
23:3 . . . . . 53, 66
23:20ff. 52
23:23 52

23:29, 35 53
23:34 . . . . 52, 54
23:38 54
24:6, 13 57
25:31–46 53
26:28 34
27:25 54
27:42 53
28:19 54
28:20 50

Mark
1:17 45
1:24f. 44
1:44 51
2:1–3:6 43
2:15ff., 23–28. . 46
3:5 65
3:16–19 . . . 45, 46
3:29 44
4:12 54
4:24f. 55
5:38 51
6:18 51
6:34–44 47
6:56 51
7:1–16 53
7:1–23 60
7:13*b* 65
7:19*b* . 46, 65, 171
7:21f. 47
8:1–9, 14–21 . . 47
8:34, 35–38 . . . 45
9:19 48
10:2–12 47
10:5 120
10:11–12 . . . 171
10:19 . . . . 46, 48
10:42–45 47
10:45 48
11:23f. 108
12:18–27, 35ff. . 45
12:28–31 46
12:31, 28–34 . . 45

13:7, 13*b* 57
13:31 49
13:32 48
13:33–37 . . 46, 47
14:14 48
14:24 . . . . 47, 48
14:62 . . . . 44, 48
16:6, 7 . . . . 44, 48

Luke
1:70ff. 61
1:72–75 61
2:21, 22, 34,
   39 59
2:30ff. 61
4:2*b*–12; 7:2–3,
   6–10. 42
4:6 129
4:16–21 57
5:14 . . . . . 51, 59
6:25 108
8:18 55
8:44 51
10:27 46
10:27–29 57
11:33–36 42
11:38–44 60
11:41 60
11:42 52
12:33 60
16:16 . . . . 51, 57
16:17, 18 60
16:29, 31 59
17:3–4, 6 42
17:14 51
18:20 . . . 46, 120
21:9, 12, 19. . . 57
24:27, 44 59
24:47 62
25:8 59

John
1:14, 16 118
1:17 . . . 117, 118

1:18 118
2:10 118
3:6, 19, 21, 27,
   31, 32. . . . 114
3:35 119
4:10 119
4:14 115
4:24 . . . 115, 121
5:21 115
5:24 115
5:45ff. 119
6:32–35, 58. . 119
7:18, 19 118
8:13, 17, 31,
   33–59. . . . 119
8:38, 40 115
8:44 128
9:5 115
9:28f. 120
9:31 119
10:18 120
10:35 . . . 51, 119
12:49f. 120
13:34 . . 120, 122
14:15, 21, 31 . 120
15:10 120
15:12 . . 120, 122
15:19, 20 . . . 115
16:11 115

Acts
1:11 57
1:16 51
2:23, 24, 39. . . 59
2:38 62
2:38ff. 57
3:25f. 61
4:12 62
4:25 51
6–7. 59
6:11, 13 59
6:14 . . . . . 59, 60
7 60
7:8 61

7:38 59
7:51 59
7:53 62
10–11 61
10:2, 4, 31 . . . 60
10:9–23 171
10:13ff. 59
10:15 46
10:25–28 60
10:28 59
10:38 57
11:3 59
13:26 62
13:38 . . . . 59, 62
13:38f., 48b . . 62
13:43 62
13:46 42
13:46f. 62
15 . . . 61, 63, 170
15:1, 5, 21 . . . 59
15:7ff., 10, 14. . 62
15:8f. 62
15:11 62
15:13–21 . . . 171
15:16, 17 61
15:20, 28–29a . 62
15:28f. 187
16:3 59
17:24–28 78
18:6 17
18:13 59
21:15–26 . . 59, 62
21:20 . 59, 60, 63
21:21–24, 28
. . . . 59, 60
22:3 . . . . . 59, 81
23:3 59
24:7 60
24:47 62
28:17 . . . . 59, 60
28:23 59

Romans
1–8. 94

1:17 74
1:18–3:20 94
1:20f. 84, 86
1:32 72
2:6ff. 167
2:13 95
2:14, 17–24 . . . 72
2:14ff. 94
2:15b 84
2:29 94
3:5, 7 95
3:9 . . . 75, 80, 91
3:10b–18 95
3:20 95
3:21 96
3:22 . . . . . 91, 95
3:23f. 75, 91
3:24–26 91
3:27, 28, 31. . . 96
3:28 111
5:1 . . . 77, 94, 97
5:6, 9, 10 97
5:12 147
5:12–19 . . . 80, 86
5:12–21 . . . 76, 97
5:14, 15,
    17f., 20 92
5:18f. 77
6:1–11, 20, 22 . 98
6:2, 4, 6, 11f. . . 76
6:3–5. 74
6:14 . . . . . 74, 84
6:16 94
6:19 77
6:20 94
7:4 . . . . . . 74, 76
7:5f. 94
7:6–11 99
7:13ff. 86
7:14 . . . . . 74, 91
7:18 75
7:22 . . . . . 83, 91
7:23, 24 100
8:1 94

8:1–11. 87
8:2–34. 100
8:3f. 75
8:13 85
8:18–21, 24, 29
. . . . 79
8:20f. 91
8:22f. . . . 84, 152
8:26f. 84
8:29 87
9–11 . . . . 42, 63,
            94, 101
9:4 . . . . . 34, 102
9:13, 15, 17,
    23–32. . . . 102
9:31f. 103
10:3 103
10:4 49
10:5–21 . . . . 102f.
11:6, 11f. . . . 103
11:7 104
11:15–31 . . . 102
11:23–28 . . . 104
12–15 94
12:1 84
12:1–15:13
. . . . . . 104, 111
12:9–21 111
13:8–10 104
16:18–20 17

1 Corinthians
1:21 84
1:30 76
2:11 83
3:8 167
6:12f. 17, 84
7:1–16, 17. . . . 85
7:28, 31 130
8:6 79
10:1–5 17
12:12 : 76
15:20ff. 76
15:20–28 86

202

15:22 80
15:35–49 81

2 Corinthians
2:13 83
3:6 34
3:13 17
4:4 . . . 85, 87, 129
5:2–5 81
5:10 167
5:17 76
5:21 . . 75, 76, 87
6:16f. 51
7:5 83
11:13ff. 17
12:11 17
13:7 148

Galatians
1:14 . . . . . 16, 74
2:2, 7f. 17
2:8 42
2:10 170
2:11–14 17
2:16, 20 77
3:1–5 93
3:3 98
3:10 . . . . 74, 111
3:14 17
3:23–27 74
4:3ff. 78, 80
4:4 94
4:8 93
4:22–26 17
5:1 93
5:14, 18 74
5:16f. 87
5:19 92
6:12 17
6:15 76

Ephesians
1:6, 14 73
1:10 79

2:2 85
4:17–24 76
6:12 86

Philippians
1:11 77
2:10 85
3:2f. 17
3:5 . . . . . 17, 81
3:5f., 7–11 . . . 87
3:6*b* 74
3:9f. 76

Colossians
1:16 85
1:18, 20 73
1:20 79
2:10 85
3:1–17 76

1 Thessalonians
2:15–16*a* 71
2:18 85

2 Thessalonians
2:7 . . . . . . 85, 87
2:9 85

1 Timothy
3:2 130
4:4 153
6:14 120

2 Timothy
3:15f. 155

Titus
1:6 130

Hebrews
7:22 34
8:6 34
9:15, 20 34

James
1:1 107
1:3–27 110
1:5 . . . . 108, 111
1:6, 9, 12,
  17, 22 108
1:18, 21 109
1:25 122
1:26f. 112
2 109
2:1 . . . . 107, 112
2:1–7 108
2:1–26 110
2:7 109
2:8ff. . . . 111, 122
2:11 112
2:14–26 . 108, 112
2:17 159
2:21f. 109
2:24 . . . 111, 113
3:1–18 110
3:17 111
4:1–17 110
4:2f., 4 112
4:7f., 11f. . . . 111
4:9, 12 108
5:1–6 . . . 108, 112
5:1–20 110
5:8 . . . . 109, 111
5:11, 12 108
5:14 109
5:15 112

1 Peter
1:18–21 166

2 Peter
1:1 122
1:1f., 5, 12 . . 114
1:3f. 139
1:4 177
2:17*b* 114
2:1–18 114
2:4, 6, 10,

14, 18. 139
2:20 122
2:21 120
3:1–3, 14, 18 . 114
3:2 . 114, 120, 122
3:15f. 155
3:18 122

1 John
4:7–21 121
5:2, 3 121

5:19 128

2 John
5 122

Jude
1 122
1–3, 9f., 14,
  20–22,
  24–25 113
1f., 3, 5, 13*b*,

4–16, 17f.,
  24, 25 114

1 Clement
27:5 49

Didache
8:1 172

Gospel of Thomas
29, 56, 87 43

SUBJECT AND AUTHOR INDEX

Abraham, 81, 82, 96f., 119. *See also* Covenant

Adam, 73, 80, 81, 82, 86, 89–91, 97, 135, 139, 140, 142–145, 147, 155f., 164f., 168, 174

Albigenses and Cathari, 158

Angels, 86, 113, 139, 140, 160

Antinomianism, 67, 98, 113

Apocrypha and Pseudepigrapha, 15, 37

Apologists, 125, 138, 139, 140, 144

Apuleius, 124, 190

Aquinas, St. Thomas, 177, 179

Armstrong, Arthur H., 183

Asceticism, Christian, 11, 130, 172

Athanasius, St., 163

Augustine, St., 102, 142f., 145–150, 164f., 193, 194

Banks, Robert, 65f., 185, 188

Baptism, 74, 108f., 141, 151, 161

Barnabas. *See* Pseudo-Barnabas

Barrett, Charles Kingsley, 116, 190

Barth, Gerhard, 56, 186, 187

Basil, St., 140, 193

Baur, Ferdinand Christian, 39

Baye, Michel du, 178

Beatitudes in James and Matthew, 108

Bornkamm, Günther, 52, 53, 186

Bowker, John, 191

Branscomb, Harvie, 65

Bultmann, Rudolf, 40, 78, 79, 83, 114, 125, 188, 191

Cain, 21, 140, 141

Caird, G. B., 189

Calvin, John, 40, 102

Cassian, John, 149f., 194

Celibacy, 11, 85, 154, 172

Chadwick, Henry, 183

Charles, R. H., 184

Chrysostom, St. John, 193

Church, 56, 60, 63, 73f., 76, 84, 88, 101, 105f., 168, 180; councils, 154, 156f., 158–160, 178; creeds, 158, 165, 180

Circumcision, 58, 59, 61

Clement, St., 193

Commandment(s), 120, 122

Conzelmann, Hans, 40, 56, 57, 187

Cooke, Bernard, 191

Cosmos: balance in, 97f.; Christ in, 73, 79; enslavement of, 100

Covenant: Abrahamic, 15, 23f., 30, 32, 61, 81, 94, 96; "book of the" (Dt 12–26; 28–30), 31; Davidic, 32; "new," "everlasting," 31f., 58; Noachide, 23, 30; as an order of grace, 44, 48f., 62, 174; relation of just deeds to, 35; renewed at Horeb-Sinai, 24ff., 31, 182; renewed under Isaac, Jacob-Israel, 24; translated as "testament," 34; wisdom literature and, 34

Creation: etiological legends about, 21; human continuity with, 155f.; human dominance in, 11; in Paul, 78f., 152; and redemption, 10, 11, 78f., 90f., 175; works of, 11, 20f., 27

Cyprian, St., 142

Dahl, Nils A., 63
Damascus Document, 16
Daniélou, Jean, 183
Daube, David, 185
Davies, W. D., 189
Deliverance from Egypt (Salvation), 22f., 25f., 32, 93, 102
Demonic: Jesus in contest with the, 43; legendary proliferation of the, 20; realm of the, 19f., 37, 68, 85f., 87, 91, 115, 129, 151, 160–162
Denzinger-Bannwart-Rahner, 194
Denzinger-Schönmetzer, 194
Discipleship, 45ff., 64, 67, 68, 74, 111, 122, 170f.
Divinization of humanity, 134, 151, 175
Dodds, Eric R., 126, 142, 191, 193
Donahue, John R., 186
Dualism: ethical, 19ff., 131, 162; in Johannine writings, 114; metaphysical, 11, 20, 112,

127f., 129, 147, 158f., 162; in Paul, 88

Ebionites ("the poor"), 108
Eichrodt, Walther, 28, 185
Eissfeldt, Otto, 22, 184
Elert, Werner, 117, 190
Elijah, 110
Enoch, 82, 113
Eon thought, Jewish, 116, 122, 180
Eschatology: as a concern of Jesus, 47; of James, 111; of Luke, 57; of Mark, 47f., 65; of Matthew, 55; of Paul, 78f.
Eucharist, 84, 172
Eve-Mary parallel, 140

Faith and works in James, 108, 109f., 111, 112f.
"Fall" of humanity, 141, 143, 151, 163, 168
Faustus of Riez, 149, 194
Festugière, A. J., 125, 190
Fitzmyer, Joseph, 187
Forgiveness, divine (in Luke), 67
Furnish, Victor Paul, 185

Gärtner, Bertil, 187
Gentiles (Greeks): as part of the covenant community, 58, 61, 62, 63, 64, 70, 73; salvation of, 79, 103f.
Gibbs, John G., 79, 188
Gnosis, pre-Christian, 125, 129, 131, 132, 135f.
Gnostics, Christian, 88, 121, 147, 156, 172
God-fearers, gentile, 9, 62, 133
Grace: creation and redemption as, 44, 69, 145; enabling, 29, 136, 137, 168, 175; God as, 29, 169, 175, 179; in John, 117;

and law, 42, 56, 75, 175; in Luke-Acts, 48; in Paul, 48, 117; as promise, fulfillment in Christ, 80f., 91, 92; St. Augustine on, 145–150; and truth (gracious truth), 12, 115, 117f.; ubiquity of, 140
Greenberg, Moshe, 184
Gregory of Palamas, 134
Gryson, Roger, 184
Guillaumont, A., 185
Guthrie, Donald, 109, 190

Haenchen, Gustav, 56, 187
Hamerton-Kelly, Robert G., 188
Hare, Douglas R. A., 186
Harnack, Adolf von, 56
Harrington, Daniel, 186
Hengel, Martin, 184, 190
Hermas, Shepherd of, 136, 139, 171, 192
Heschel, Abraham J., 25, 184
Hillel, 81
History-of-religions school, 125, 132
Holiness Code of Leviticus, 32
Holy Spirit (Paraclete), 113, 122, 137, 148
Hooker, Richard, 177, 194
Hubbard, B. J., 186
Human capacities, acts, 49, 53, 67, 68, 83, 84, 89, 94, 99, 100, 111, 112, 124, 135, 139, 141, 149, 153, 166f., 178
Humani Generis, 178

Iavneh, academy at, 50, 52
Ignatius of Antioch, St., 136, 138, 193
Irenaeus, St., 136, 137, 140, 143f., 183, 192, 193

Jacob, Edmund, 185
Jerusalem, destruction of, 47, 57, 59
Jervell, Jacob, 56, 58, 63, 187, 188
Jesus as observant Jew, 64, 66
Jewish Christians (Christian Jews), 61, 63, 64, 65, 72, 120
Job, 110, 130
Johanan ben Zakkai, 87, 124, 170
John the Baptist, 37, 51, 114
Josephus, 16, 107, 184, 189
Judah ha Nasi (the Patriarch), 87, 170
Judaism, Jews, 10, 11, 13, 15, 71ff., 169, 172f., 181; apocalyptic, 16, 64f., 81, 113, 132; Creator-creature distinction in, 87; divine sanction on works in, 136; God's love for, in Paul, 102, 174; Hellenized, 36, 58, 81, 86, 87, 111, 115, 124; hope proper to, 152; legal outlook of, 137; polemic against, in John, 121; rabbinic, 29, 79f., 81f., 91, 93f., 111, 120, 124; "re-Judaizing" of Christianity, 172; response of, in Matthew, 54; response of, in Paul, 71f., 101, 102, 106
Judgment, future, 42, 55, 84
Juel, Donald, 185
Justin Martyr, St., 138, 139, 140, 171, 192f.

Käsemann, Ernst, 54f., 80, 84, 187, 188
Kaufmann, Yehezkel, 184, 191
Keck, Leander, 187, 189
Kee, Howard Clark, 7, 42, 185
Kelly, J. N. D., 11, 184
Knox, John, 66f., 188
Kümmel, W. G., 189

Lange-James theory, 99

Law, Christian message expressed by, 9, 49f., 55, 56, 67, 74, 101, 104, 120

Law, Mosaic, 15, 16, 25, 27, 29, 37, 153; ethical vis à vis ceremonial, legal, 57; "fulfilling," in Matthew, 49f., 52; fulfillment of by human effort, 77; fulfillment of, in John, 116ff., 119, 123; fully kept by Luke's Christian Jews, 63; as a gift of God, 118, 174; Jesus' concern for, 48, 66; Jesus as true interpreter of, 50f., 63, 69; justification by, 77, 92f., 95, 97; parts of oral Law not binding, 46, 52, 53; as "perfect law of freedom," "kingly law," 109, 122, 171; in Priestly writings, 32; rabbinic interpretation of, 43, 49, 50, 170; as summing up covenant demands, 36, 59f.; as supplanted by the gospel, 38, 74, 92f.; still binding for Christians, 46, 52, 60, 62, 69f., 171; Ten Words (Ten Commandments), 26, 28, 117; unfavorable disposition of Synoptics toward, 45; zeal for, in Chronicles, Ezra, Nehemiah, 32f.

Law, William, 194, 195

Lofthouse, W. F., 184

Lubac, Henri de, 178, 194, 195

Luther, Martin, 109

Mach, R., 189

Marcionite tendency, 46, 50, 56, 131, 172

Marcus Aurelius, 126, 127

Markus, Robert A., 183

Marmorstein, Arthur, 189

Marriage, sexuality and, 85, 90, 130, 154

Martyrdom, 142

Matter, 21, 42, 112, 153, 158f.

McKenzie, John L., 189

Mendenhall, George, 185

Meyer, A., 107, 189

Mishnah and Talmud, 18, 33

Monarchy, Davidic, 28

Moore, George Foot, 186, 191

Moses, 81, 82, 116; body of, 113; type of Christ in John, 119

Muslims, 11, 172

Myers, Jacob M., 30, 184, 189

Mythology and the Bible, 18f.

Nag Hamâdi, Coptic library of, 39, 43

Nature: as good, 68, 154, 158, 181; contrasted with grace, 9f., 153; human, balance in, 167; in Paul, 78, 88, 89

New age in Christ, 73, 78, 80, 81, 116

Noachian precepts, 82, 94, 140, 141

Nock, Arthur Darby, 125, 190, 191

Oaths, 110

Origen, 135, 192, 193

Overbeck, Franz, 56

Pagels, Elaine, 188, 190

Parables of Jesus, 48, 51, 54, 57, 67

Parousia, 44, 57, 111, 180

Passover, 22, 65

Paul, St.: in Acts, 59f., 62; atonement for sins absent from, 93f.; autobiographical soliloquy in, 83, 99f.; boastfulness in, 83; body in, 84f.; cosmic struggle in, 83, 91; discontinuity in, 80f.; dualism in, 88; eon thought in, 81, 82, 97, 99, 101, 103, 105; epistles of, 38f., 70, 136, 141, 155, 171; esteem for the Law in, 104; essential Jewishness of, 105; figure of slavery in, 94, 98; "flesh" in, 74, 75, 83, 84, 86f., 91; God's love for humanity in, 68, 96; God's love for Jews in, 102, 174; identifying opponents of, 17f.; idolatry in, 83; "image of God" in, 87; "image of his son" in, 79; and individuals, 83, 92, 98; justification, justifying faith in, 62, 71, 74f., 76f., 80, 87, 92, 94f., 96; the Law as expendable for, 70, 71, 74, 170, 175; Law-justification in, 77, 92, 94f., 97, 170; law of sin vs. law of grace, 101; mythic structures in, 105f.; predestination in, 100, 102; relation to Jews and Gentiles, 17, 70, 170; self-perception of, 16f.; sin in, 89–100; slow acceptance of, 40; "spirit" in, 83, 84f., 86f.; tension between Synoptics and, 39, 41f.

Pelagius, 142f., 150, 193

Pelikan, Jaroslav, 150, 192, 194

Persecution of Christians, 54, 57

Pharisees, 16f., 30, 45, 49, 52, 53f., 64, 67, 81

Philo, 90, 132, 169, 171, 184

Philoponus, John, 191

Plato and Platonism, 115, 127, 191

Potterie, Ignace de la, 190

Proclus, 126

Prophets: opposition to monarchy by, 28f.; return to Torah supported by, 28, 67; social

teaching of, 112; supposed opposition to the Law, 27f.

Prosper of Aquitaine, 150, 194

Pseudo-Barnabas, 136, 138, 171, 192, 193

Pseudo-Dionysius, 177

"Q" sayings, 39, 41, 42, 51, 58, 166

Qumrân community, 16, 88, 132, 169; Dead Sea scrolls of, 35f., 53

Reformers, 12, 70f.

Reign of God (Kingdom of God), 44, 48, 69, 79, 181

Resurrection: of Jesus, 73, 82, 166; of the just, 81, 100, 180

Rich and poor in James, 110

Righteous Teacher, 16, 35, 37, 171

Righteousness (justice): of God in Paul vis-à-vis ethical, 75f., 94, 104; God's forgiveness as highest, 67; higher, 49, 50, 53, 60, 171; original, 144

Robinson, John A. T., 109

Sabbath observance, 27, 30, 43, 51

Sacrifice (spiritual worship), 104

Sadducees, 79

Salvation: by Christ's blood, 166; through divine wisdom taught by Jesus, 48, 166; as restoration in the final age, 78, 87, 177f. See also Deliverance

Sambursky, Samuel, 191

Sanders, E. P., 189

Sanders, Jack T., 46, 186

Satan (devil), 19, 42, 85, 113, 115, 128, 129, 140, 145, 151, 159–162

Schmithals, Walter, 45, 184, 185

Schoeps, H. J., 183

Scotus Erigena, 177

Scroggs, Robin, 188, 189, 194

Scullion, J. J., 189

Self-revelation, God's, 10f., 12, 118, 120, 175

Septuagint, 34, 59, 74, 107, 117, 136, 154

Sin, 21, 68, 72f., 75, 80, 87, 89–100, 141–149, 167f.; as distinct from sins, 72, 92, 95, 97; original, 80, 89, 90f., 135, 142, 164; sins (transgressions), 110, 111

Sloyan, Gerard S., 189

Socrates, 135

Son of man, 55, 82

Speiser, E. A., 189

Spirit: implanted gift of, at creation, 140; in relation to the Law, 27, 74

Spitta, Friedrich, 107

Stinson, Charles, 179, 184, 195

Stoic philosophy, 135

Supernatural, 12, 177–179

Tatian, 135, 139, 144, 192

Temple sacrifice, 28, 93, 116

Tertullian, 193

Theophilus, 139, 144, 193

Torah (Mosaic books), 18, 21, 25, 29, 31, 81

Torrance, Thomas F., 136, 137, 192

Toynbee, Arnold, 183

Trilling, Wolfgang, 186

Twofold commandment, 45, 46f., 57, 67, 120f., 171

Two-sphere universe, 12, 114, 115

"Watchers" ("giants" of Gn 6), 19, 89, 139, 151

Watson, E. W., 142, 193

Weidenfeld, M., 185

Wellhausen, Julius, 27, 185

Werner, Martin, 66

Wilson, Stephen G., 63, 187

Windisch, Hans, 65

Wisdom, pagan, 80

Wolff, Hans Werner, 27, 185

"Works of the Law," 12, 74, 96, 137, 174f.

Yom Kippur, 93

Zaehner, R. C., 129, 191

Ziesler, J. A., 76f., 188, 189

Zoroastrian religion, 128, 129f.